Monetary Policies - Theories, Empirics, Myths, and Realities

Edited by Chee-Heong Quah and Say Wah Lee

Published in London, United Kingdom

Monetary Policies - Theories, Empirics, Myths, and Realities
http://dx.doi.org/10.5772/intechopen.1010530
Edited by Chee-Heong Quah and Say Wah Lee

Contributors
Anita Rani Chopra, Ashok Chopra, Basma Almisshal, Chee-Heong Quah, Chee Heong Quah, Dieter Lichtenstein, Yew Joe Ho

First published in London, United Kingdom, 2026 by IntechOpen
IntechOpen is the global imprint of INTECHOPEN LIMITED, registered in England and Wales, registration number: 11086078, 167-169 Great Portland Street, London, W1W 5PF, United Kingdom

For EU product safety concerns: IN TECH d.o.o., Prolaz Marije Krucifikse Kozulić 3, 51000 Rijeka, Croatia, info@intechopen.com or visit our website at intechopen.com.

British Library Cataloguing-in-Publication Data
A catalogue record for this book is available from the British Library

Monetary Policies - Theories, Empirics, Myths, and Realities
Edited by Chee-Heong Quah and Say Wah Lee
p. cm.

This title is part of the Business, Management and Economics Book Series, Volume 54
Topic: Economics
Series Editor: Taufiq Choudhry
Topic Editor: Jaime Ortiz

Print ISBN 978-1-80631-715-8
Online ISBN 978-1-80631-714-1
eBook (PDF) ISBN 978-1-80631-716-5
ISSN 2753-894X

IntechOpen Book Series

Business, Management and Economics

Volume 54

Aims and Scope of the Series

This series will provide a comprehensive overview of recent research trends in business and management, economics, and marketing. Topics will include asset liability management, financial consequences of the financial crisis and covid-19, financial accounting, mergers and acquisitions, management accounting, SMEs, financial markets, corporate finance and governance, managerial technology and innovation, resource management and sustainable development, social entrepreneurship, corporate responsibility, ethics and accountability, microeconomics, labour economics, macroeconomics, public economics, financial economics, econometrics, direct marketing, creative marketing, internet marketing, market planning and forecasting, brand management, market segmentation and targeting and other topics under business and management. This book series will focus on various aspects of business and management whose in-depth understanding is critical for business and company management to function effectively during this uncertain time of financial crisis, Covid-19 pandemic, and military activity in Europe.

Meet the Series Editor

Prof. Choudhry holds a BSc degree in Economics from the University of Iowa, as well as a Masters and Ph.D. in Applied Economics from Clemson University, USA. In January 2006, he became a Professor of Finance at the University of Southampton Business School. He was previously a Professor of Finance at the University of Bradford Management School. He has over 80 articles published in international finance and economics journals. His research interests and specialties include financial econometrics, financial economics, international economics and finance, housing markets, financial markets, among others.

Meet the Volume Editors

Chee-Heong Quah, Ph.D., is an academic at the Faculty of Business and Economics, University of Malaya. His research interests encompass international economics, monetary integration, financial crisis, optimum currency areas, and Austrian economics. His works have been published in scientific journals such as *Asia Pacific Business Review; International Finance; Journal of Business, Economics, and Management; Journal of the Asia Pacific Economy; Actual Economic Problems; African Journal of Business and Management; South Asian Journal of Management*; and *International Journal of Asia Pacific Studies.*

Lee Say Wah (Sarah) is a senior lecturer in the Faculty of Business and Economics, Universiti Malaya, Malaysia. She earned her Ph.D. from Shanghai Jiao Tong University, China. Dr. Lee has published several papers in the Web of Science (WOS) and Scopus. She specializes in consumer behavior and quantitative studies.

Contents

Preface

The effectiveness and efficiency of centralized policy, including state intervention in the realms of money, have long been a subject of debate amongst scholars and practitioners alike. The pro-intervention schools, namely the Keynesian school, the Modern Monetary Theory school, and the Marxist/socialist school, assert that money is too important a commodity to be left to the invisible hands of the free market. Meanwhile, the monetarist Chicago school, led by Milton Friedman, advocates steady, predictable growth of the money supply that is independent of the whims of the state. Still, free-market schools such as the Austrian school stress that centralized, one-size-fits-all controls over the ever-critical consumption and investment good of money will only bring about more harm than good, because the state cannot possibly replace the decentralized decisions of millions of actors in the economy, including those involving money. Only demand and supply, and the resulting prices of money and interest rates across markets, can lead decision-makers to the best possible outcomes in terms of effectiveness and efficiency for individuals.

This book collects theoretical argumentative discourses and applied empirical studies to advance once again the arguments behind the differences between these schools of thought. An exploration into cryptocurrency, a recent product of the money market, is also presented against the principles of the schools of thought. Readers of this title will find it enlightening and invigorating, as it delivers classical, practical ideas in a light that today's generation has never seen before.

Chee-Heong Quah and Say-Wah Lee
Faculty of Business and Economics,
University of Malaya,
Kuala Lumpur, Malaysia

Chapter 1

Introductory Chapter: A Response to Michael Spence

Chee Heong Quah

1. Introduction

In his commentary "Why Are Supply Chains Blocked?" [1], Michael Spence[1], the Nobel laureate in economics at Stanford University, explains the reasons behind the supply chain disruptions that took place in the US in the fall of 2021. The first reasons cited in the article are expansionary monetary policy, high savings and repressed demand during lockdowns and the pandemic, and massive fiscal spending by the government.

Nonetheless, a fundamental question needs to be asked: Could this fiasco have happened in a world that substantially adheres to the prescriptions of Austrian economics? To be clear, this world, centered on Austrian principles [2], the hypothetical Austrian world as an analytic tool used here, is fully laissez-faire. Hence, there would be no role for the government in money, if there is any government at all.

2. Will there be monetary inflation in a truly free economy?

Since monetary inflation has been commonly cited as the predominant factor behind the supply chain blockage, it is compelling to delve into the money sphere. With respect to money, a couple of arrangements in the money market may emerge in the Austrian world [3]. In one of the arrangements, there will be free banking, namely an economy with private banks competing with each other by issuing their own brands of money and related services. This scenario is not much different from our current world, in which smartphone companies and credit card issuers compete with each other for customers and market share in an economy. If these markets in our current world can foretell, in the Austrian world, eventually, in the long run, there would remain a few, probably two or three, dominant issuers of money, each with a certain degree of monopolistic power.

Of course, in a completely free market, banks and money issuers can also be independent entities depending on the net marginal benefits of alternate arrangements of firms [4]. In the credit card services market today, the three major brands worldwide are Visa, MasterCard, and American Express. In the smartphone

[1] Michael Spence, a Nobel laureate in economics, is Professor of Economics Emeritus and a former dean of the Graduate School of Business at Stanford University. He is Senior Fellow at the Hoover Institution, serves on the Academic Committee at Luohan Academy, and co-chairs the Advisory Board of the Asia Global Institute.

IntechOpen

market, the three dominant players globally are none other than Samsung, Apple, and Huawei. Of course, specific dominant players do change from time to time, but it can be certain to argue that, in the long run, a small number of suppliers will sustain in every niche of the broader money market. Each of the dominant brands mentioned above has to compete in the global marketplace, where essentially there is no one central government of the entire planet to protect it from competition. In our current world, the global market is relatively free when compared to domestic markets. While in home markets, large firms are able to seek favors from local lawmakers relatively easily, the same firms must compete politically with each other and with home country firms across the many countries if they wish to seek political favors from lawmakers of so many countries in the world to be globally dominant.

Suppose indeed there are two or three money issuers with monopolistic powers, would the money market in the Austrian world resemble what we now have in our current world? Possibly to some extent, yes, but what is certain in the Austrian world, with an unhampered free market minus any government interference in the money market, is that circumstances would be a lot better. The million-dollar question is whether money would still lose value or lose it at a rate as rapid as what we are now experiencing when there is no central bank nor government meddling. To recollect, price inflation or diminishing value of money or falling purchasing power happens when too much money or too many dollars are chasing after too few goods. Of course, empirically, it involves a loss of purchasing power over a wide range of, but not all, products and services, and the decrease keeps going on over a long, sustained period of time. Theoretically, however, when money grows much faster than goods and services, money shall lose value over all goods and services. The empirical observation that money does not lose purchasing power against certain goods despite money growing faster than all goods does not mean that price inflation has not occurred; it simply means that other factor or factors in the real world have offset the effect of the falling value of money.

Unlike in our present world, where the central bank enjoys monopoly power over the supply of legal tender, in the Austrian world, private money issuers have to compete against each other for customers to use their respective monies and services. On top of that, they also need to compete against money substitutes such as precious metals, private barter exchanges, online money substitutes, and other innovative private arrangements between individuals and organizations, which could substitute for money, banking, and financial services.

3. Competition in money

As the law of competition always holds [5], the greater the competition between the sellers, the greater the value per dollar received by consumers, all other things constant. If most consumers value a stable or rising value of money over time, the money issuers would have no choice but to raise the value of their issued monies over time, even though they might be tempted to increase money supplies to lend out as loans. In a free society setting, a couple of scenarios can be conjectured.

In the scenario where most consumers value stable or rising purchasing power of money, the money issuers would restrict and might even refrain from issuing new money altogether. Since goods and services increase over time as society, technology, and production progress, the value of money would increase against all goods and services in the long run. Money issuers who attempt to increase supply, where early receivers of money gain at the expense of later recipients of that money, would be driven out of business as customers learn that these monies lose purchasing power. In this scenario, a couple of monies would circulate in the economy and be used as a store of value, medium of exchange, and unit of account. The ones that survive in the market would be those with stable or increasing value.

In the long run, businesses and retailers would only accept certain reliable brands of money, and so would consumers. When most people accept only certain brands of money, the rest of the brands would be driven out of circulation due to network effects, so that eventually one, two, or three issuers would remain. If a brand of money manages to monopolize the market, begins to increase the money supply, and devalues at a rate not acceptable to most users, other issuers would begin to enter the market because there is no barrier to entry at all. As competition sets in, all brands of money would make sure their monies offer what is valued by users or money consumers, namely stable or rising purchasing power. In short, the forces of competition will ensure a reasonable quality of money is produced by issuers in the unhampered money market.

It is then up to consumers to decide, just like in any other market, what constitutes quality for money as a consumer good, and what is of value. It is completely comprehensible if a certain brand of issuer creates value for its segment of customers by offering easier credit that comes with greater money supply. Alternatively, an issuer can also offer benefits such as ease of use to attract certain portions of the population. In the free market, there is no one identical set of strategies for all producers and sellers; it is up to entrepreneurs to decide on what kinds of strategies they want to employ. Generally, money issuers can employ a combination of differentiation and cost leadership strategies to cater to their respective customer segments.

In the Austrian world, issuers can choose to back their money supplies with precious metals such as gold and silver, or any valuable assets such as stocks, real property, or jewels. Issuers can even back their money with bonds and bills offered by private firms and governments. There can even be no backing at all, or backing based on reputation and branding. There is simply no limitation to the nature of the money issued, and it is up to the imagination and creativity of entrepreneurs to figure out what to offer to satisfy their customers. In this unfettered market, the basic non-aggression principle applies, such that it is legal for anyone to do anything he or she wants, provided that he or she does not initiate or threaten violence against any person or legitimately owned property of another.

In short, in this scenario, where there are multiple private issuers of money, there may still be monetary inflation, but it will be restricted as it only affects monies and money users of certain brands of money that inflate their money supplies excessively and arbitrarily.

Author details

Chee Heong Quah
Faculty of Business and Economics, University of Malaya, Kuala Lumpur, Malaysia

*Address all correspondence to: quahch@um.edu.my

References

[1] Spence M. Why Are Supply Chains Blocked? 2021, November 3. Project Syndicate. Available from: https://www.project-syndicate.org/commentary/prevent-future-supply-chain-disruptions-using-ai-models-by-michael-spence-2021-11/english#comments [Accessed: 2021-November-4]

[2] Quah CH. Austrian Economics in One Lesson. Manipal, India: Manipal Universal Press; 2021

[3] Mayer T. Austrian Economics, Money and Finance. London, United Kingdom: Routledge; 2017

[4] Selgin GA, White LH. The evolution of a free banking system. Economic Inquiry. 1987;**25**(3):439–457

[5] Wandel J. Competition and antitrust policy: An Austrian economics perspective. Progress in Economics Research. Nueva York: Nova Publishers. 2015;**30**:47–60

Chapter 2

Rethinking Monetary Policy: Theory, Evidence and Institutional Constraints

Ashok Chopra and Anita Rani Chopra

Abstract

Monetary policy remains a central component of macroeconomic management, influencing inflation, output, and financial stability through interventions in interest rates, liquidity, and credit conditions. This chapter presents an integrated analysis of the theoretical foundations, empirical evidence, and practical constraints shaping monetary policy across advanced, emerging, and regionally specific economies. It traces the evolution of monetary thought from Classical and Monetarist neutrality doctrines to the New Keynesian emphasis on nominal rigidities and short-run non-neutrality, highlighting the differing assumptions and policy implications associated with each framework. Empirical evidence indicates that monetary policy produces measurable short-run effects on inflation and output, while its long-run influence is constrained by structural factors and expectations. Experiences from advanced economies, including the United States, the Eurozone, and Japan, show that post-crisis unconventional measures such as quantitative easing, forward guidance, and yield-curve control lowered long-term yields and stabilized financial markets but also contributed to asset-price inflation and distributional concerns. In contrast, emerging markets exhibit weaker and more volatile transmission due to fiscal dominance, limited financial depth, and exchange-rate constraints. The experience of Gulf Cooperation Council economies, particularly the United Arab Emirates, illustrates the trade-off between constrained monetary autonomy under a U.S. dollar peg and the benefits of exchange-rate stability. The chapter critically examines persistent misconceptions regarding central bank capabilities, demonstrating that money creation is largely endogenous, employment outcomes depend on structural conditions, and monetary policy operates within fiscal and political constraints. It further examines emerging challenges associated with digitalization, climate-related risks, and macroprudential regulation. The chapter concludes that monetary policy is both influential and inherently limited, requiring credible institutions, transparent communication, and coordination with fiscal and structural policies to remain effective in an increasingly interconnected global economy.

Keywords: monetary policy, central banking, inflation targeting, quantitative easing, interest rate transmission, financial stability, monetary policy myths, policy credibility, global monetary systems, Austrian business cycle theory, monetary transmission mechanisms, fiscal dominance, unconventional monetary policy, exchange rate regimes, emerging market monetary policy

1. Introduction

1.1 Concept and objectives of monetary policy

Monetary policy refers to the set of actions undertaken by a country's central bank to regulate the supply of money, the availability of credit, and the level of interest rates to achieve macroeconomic stability. It is one of the two principal tools of macroeconomic management, the other being fiscal policy. The operational design and effectiveness of monetary policy depend on the institutional structure of the financial system, the legal mandate of the central bank, and the responsiveness of markets to policy signals [1].

1.2 Definition and core framework

The International Monetary Fund [2] defines monetary policy as "the process by which the monetary authority of a country controls the supply of money, often targeting an inflation rate or interest rate to ensure price stability and general trust in the currency." In practice, the policy operates through a transmission mechanism that links policy instruments – such as the policy rate, reserve requirements, and open-market operations (OMOs) – to final objectives, including inflation, employment, and growth.

The typical transmission process occurs through several interconnected channels:

A. Interest-rate channel: central-bank rate adjustments affect borrowing costs, investment, and consumption.

B. Credit channel: bank balance-sheet conditions and lending standards transmit policy impulses to private credit.

C. Exchange-rate channel: policy changes influence capital flows and currency values, affecting trade competitiveness.

D. Asset-price channel: shifts in equity and bond prices alter household wealth and corporate financing conditions.

E. The time lags between policy action and economic effect vary across economies, usually ranging from four to eight quarters [3].

1.3 Objectives and policy mandates

Central banks pursue several key objectives that reflect their statutory mandates and the macroeconomic environment.

1.3.1 Price stability

Price stability remains the principal and most universal goal of monetary policy. Persistent inflation or deflation distorts price signals, erodes purchasing power, and hampers long-term investment planning. Empirical studies indicate that maintaining low and predictable inflation promotes higher real growth by reducing uncertainty [4]. Most advanced economies have adopted explicit or implicit inflation targets – commonly around 2% – to anchor expectations [5, 6].

1.3.2 Full employment and output stabilization

Although the relationship between inflation and employment has evolved over time, the Phillips-curve framework still guides short-term stabilization policies. In dual-mandate regimes, such as that of the US Federal Reserve, monetary authorities seek to minimize deviations of output and employment from potential levels while maintaining price stability [7]. During economic contractions, an expansionary stance supports aggregate demand; conversely, during overheating, contractionary measures temper inflationary pressures.

1.3.3 Exchange-rate stability

For small open economies, exchange-rate management is a vital component of monetary stability. Pegged or managed exchange-rate regimes constrain independent monetary action but can reduce currency volatility and inflationary import shocks. Countries in the Gulf Cooperation Council (GCC), including the United Arab Emirates, peg their currencies to the US dollar, implying that domestic interest-rate movements largely mirror those of the US Federal Reserve [2].

1.3.4 Financial-system stability

Modern central banking extends beyond macroeconomic variables to encompass systemic financial stability. Liquidity support, lender-of-last-resort operations, and macro-prudential supervision form integral parts of the policy framework [8]. Following the global financial crisis of 2008, monetary authorities incorporated financial-stability indicators – such as credit-growth differentials and asset-price misalignments – into their policy assessments.

1.3.5 Economic growth and development

While monetary policy cannot permanently raise potential output, it can create conditions conducive to investment and productivity through stable financial intermediation. Empirical analyses for emerging markets show that moderate inflation, typically between 3% and 5%, correlates with optimal growth outcomes [9].

1.4 Types of monetary policy

Expansionary monetary policy:
Implemented through lower policy rates, reduced reserve ratios, or asset purchases, expansionary policy aims to stimulate borrowing and

spending during recessions. It increases the money supply and lowers the cost of credit.

1.4.1 Contractionary monetary policy

Used to restrain inflation, it raises policy rates or decreases system liquidity through open-market sales or higher reserve requirements.

1.4.2 Neutral (maintenance) policy

Adopted when the economy operates near potential output, with interest rates kept at equilibrium levels that neither stimulate nor restrain demand [10].

Empirical evidence shows that well-timed counter-cyclical policies can reduce output volatility without compromising long-term price stability [11].

1.5 Institutional design and independence

Central-bank independence (CBI) is a cornerstone of credible policy. Studies find that higher legal and operational independence correlates with lower and more stable inflation rates (Cukierman, 1992 [12]). Independence can be goal-oriented (freedom to define objectives) or instrument-oriented (autonomy in selecting tools). However, complete independence rarely exists; governments often retain ultimate authority over macroeconomic coordination, particularly in fiscal crises [13].

In emerging markets, fiscal dominance – where large public deficits pressure the central bank to accommodate debt issuance – remains a recurring challenge. This phenomenon dilutes the effectiveness of interest-rate policies and can lead to inflationary financing [14].

1.6 Transmission lags and policy effectiveness

The delayed impact of policy changes, often termed inside and outside lags, complicates stabilization efforts. Inside lags arise from recognition and decision delays; outside lags reflect the time it takes for policy actions to influence spending and prices. Quantitative studies indicate that these lags vary between industrial and developing economies, depending on financial-market depth and the credibility of the central bank [15].

Effectiveness also depends on the expectations channel: if agents anticipate central-bank actions, the policy's real effect diminishes – a concept formalized in the rational-expectations hypothesis [16].

1.7 Trade-offs and policy constraints

The coexistence of multiple objectives often creates trade-offs. Pursuing aggressive output stabilization can conflict with price stability when supply shocks occur. In open economies, the impossible trinity – a fixed exchange rate, capital mobility, and independent monetary policy – means only two of these objectives can be simultaneously achieved [17].

Central banks mitigate such constraints through communication strategies, forward guidance, and credibility-building frameworks that align market expectations with policy intentions [18].

1.8 Global and regional context

Globally, the evolution of monetary policy has transitioned from monetary-aggregate targeting in the 1970s to interest-rate rules and inflation targeting in subsequent decades. The US Federal Reserve employs a dual-mandate approach; the European Central Bank (ECB) emphasizes price stability within the Eurozone; and the Bank of Japan (BoJ) utilizes yield-curve control to sustain low borrowing costs.

In the GCC region, monetary policy operates under the constraint of dollar pegs. Despite limited discretion, regional central banks, including the Central Bank of the UAE, use liquidity-management instruments – such as certificates of deposit and repo facilities – to stabilize domestic money markets and support nonoil sector growth [2].

These structural variations highlight how institutional mandates and exchange-rate arrangements shape the design and transmission of policy across economies.

2. Theoretical foundations

Monetary policy theory has evolved significantly over the past century. Each school of thought offers distinct assumptions, mechanisms, and policy prescriptions. The primary theoretical frameworks include Classical, Keynesian, Monetarist, New Classical, and New Keynesian perspectives. **Table 1** summarizes these major approaches.

Theory	Core assumptions	Policy implications	Expected effects on economy
Classical	Money is neutral in long run; prices are flexible; markets clear	Limited role for active policy; money supply primarily influences prices	Nominal variables change; real output unaffected
Keynesian	Prices/wages sticky in short run; demand drives output	Active monetary policy can stabilize output; interest rates affect investment	Short-run influence on employment and output; policy effective during recessions
Monetarist	Money is the main driver of inflation; long-term neutrality	Rule-based, steady money supply growth	Inflation controlled; output may temporarily respond to monetary changes
New Classical	Rational expectations; agents anticipate policy	Systematic policy cannot influence real output	Only unexpected shocks affect the real economy; policy is neutral if anticipated
New Keynesian	Price/wage rigidities exist with rational expectations	Central banks can influence short-term output via interest rate rules	Short-run nonneutrality; Taylor-rule policies recommended

Sources: 18, 15, 19, 1

Table 1.
Major theoretical perspectives on monetary policy.

2.1 Classical monetary theory

The Classical school posits that money primarily affects nominal variables, leaving real output unaffected in the long run. The **quantity theory of money (QTM)** is the foundation of classical monetary theory:

$$MV = PY$$

where:

- M = money supply
- V = velocity of money
- P = price level
- Y = real output

According to 18, inflation results from excessive money growth relative to output. Classical theory implies that central banks cannot sustainably influence employment or real GDP.

2.2 Keynesian monetary framework

20 emphasized the **liquidity preference theory**, asserting that money demand depends on interest rates and income. In this framework:

$$L = f(Y, i)$$

Where L is liquidity preference, Y is income, and i is the interest rate. Monetary policy influences output through investment and consumption channels. Empirical studies show that during recessions, interest rate reductions can stimulate demand, but liquidity traps may limit effectiveness [10].

2.3 Monetarism

Monetarists, led by Friedman Friedman [19], advocate **rules-based policy**, emphasizing that erratic monetary expansions or contractions cause inflation and instability. Key principles include:

- Money supply should grow at a constant rate, aligned with potential output growth.
- Short-term deviations affect output, but in the long run, money remains neutral.

Empirical evidence from the USA in the 1970s supports monetarist predictions of persistent inflation due to loose monetary policy [Bernanke and Mishkin, 1992 [20]].

2.4 New classical and rational expectations

Lucas [16] introduced the **rational expectations hypothesis**, asserting that agents anticipate central-bank actions. Consequently:

- Systematic monetary policy cannot influence real output in the long run.
- Only unanticipated policy shocks affect the real economy.

This perspective underpins **policy credibility** concepts: predictable policies reduce economic volatility but limit discretionary short-term interventions.

2.5 New Keynesian economics

New Keynesians integrate nominal rigidities with rational expectations. Key contributions include:

- **Price and wage stickiness:** prevents instantaneous market clearing.
- **Monetary nonneutrality:** central banks can temporarily affect output.
- **Policy rules (Taylor-type rules):** the policy rate depends on inflation deviations and the output gap:

$$i_t = r + \pi_t + \alpha(\pi_t - \pi) + \beta(y_t - y)$$

where i_t = nominal policy rate $r = neutralrealrate$, π_t = current inflation, π = target inflation, y_t = actual output, y= potential output.

Empirical studies of the USA, Eurozone, and Japan indicate short-term output responsiveness to interest rate changes, confirming nonneutrality [10, 21].

3. Instruments of monetary policy

Monetary policy instruments (refer to **Table 2**) are categorized as conventional and unconventional.

Instrument	Mechanism	Short-term effect	Long-term effect
Policy rate	Changes borrowing costs	Stimulates or restrains credit	Neutral in long run
OMOs	Adjust liquidity	Immediate market liquidity impact	Supports rate targets
Reserve requirement	Bank lending capacity	Restrains or encourages lending	Affects money multiplier
QE	Buy long-term assets	Lowers yields, boosts prices	Potential financial stability risk
Forward guidance	Signals expectations	Alters investment and consumption	Strengthens credibility
Negative rates	Penalizes excess reserves	Encourages lending	Bank profitability risk
Sources: [10, 18, 22]			

Table 2.
Summary of monetary policy instruments.

3.1 Conventional tools

- Policy interest rate: determines the cost of funds in interbank and commercial markets.
- OMOs: buying/selling government securities to inject or absorb liquidity.
- Reserve requirements: mandated reserves influence banks' lending capacity.

3.2 Unconventional tools

Post-2008, central banks employed unconventional instruments:
Quantitative easing (QE): large-scale purchase of long-term assets.
Forward guidance: communicating future policy paths to influence expectations.
Negative interest rates/yield curve control: encouraging credit expansion in low-rate environments [18, 23].

In MENA, digital interoperability faces additional constraints, including limited open data frameworks and diverse regulatory landscapes across countries. The UAE's Digital Government Strategy promotes a unified digital identity and service integration framework [7] (Chopra, A, and Chopra, AR (2025), while Saudi Arabia's Yesser Program facilitates interoperability through the government service bus (GSB), a middleware platform that enables cross-entity integration. GSB functions as a centralized integration hub that connects disparate government entities, enabling them to exchange data and interact seamlessly through standardized interfaces and protocols. It acts as a secure channel through which electronic services (e-services) are delivered, orchestrated, and monitored. GSB eliminates the need for point-to-point integration by enabling agencies to publish and consume services via a shared infrastructure, reducing duplication and improving scalability. This architecture supports real-time communication, simplifies legacy system integration, and promotes data consistency across ministries and public agencies. Moreover, GSB incorporates robust authentication, logging, and service-level management features, aligning with Saudi Arabia's Vision 2030 to build a unified and digitally capable public sector.

4. Empirical evidence

Empirical research shows the heterogeneous effectiveness of monetary policy across regions.

4.1 Developed economies (USA, Eurozone, Japan)

USA: post-2008 QE reduced long-term yields by ~ 100–150 basis points and stimulated equity markets [24].

Eurozone: negative rates increased lending but compressed bank margins; inflation remained below target for extended periods [25].

Japan: yield-curve control stabilized 10-year yields at ~ 0%, yet real GDP growth remained subdued due to structural constraints [23].

Region	Policy tool	Observed effect	Transmission lag	Notes
USA	QE and rate cuts	Lower long-term yields, equity rise	2–4 quarters	Stimulated consumption
Eurozone	Negative rates	Lending ↑, bank profits ↓	3–6 quarters	Inflation below target
Japan	Yield curve control	Stabilized yields, limited GDP effect	3–5 quarters	Structural constraints
Emerging markets	Rate cuts	Inflation ↓, output effect limited	4–8 quarters	Fiscal dominance
UAE/GCC	Liquidity operations	Short-term stability	1–2 quarters	Dollar peg limits autonomy

Sources: [2, 23–25]

Table 3.
Empirical policy outcomes by region.

4.2 Emerging markets

Transmission is weaker due to shallow financial markets, currency volatility, and fiscal constraints [9]. Example: India's 2016 inflation-targeting framework stabilized CPI inflation around 4–5%, but output growth remained volatile [26].

4.3 Regional/GCC perspective

Dollar-peg regimes (UAE, Saudi Arabia) restrict independent monetary adjustments. Policy focuses on domestic liquidity and supports nonoil sectors through repo operations (refer to **Table 3**) and certificate of deposit facilities [2].

5. Myths of monetary policy

Monetary policy is widely misunderstood in both academic and public discourse. Several pervasive myths distort perceptions of central-bank capabilities, often leading to unrealistic expectations regarding macroeconomic outcomes. **Table 4** summarizes common myths and corresponding realities.

5.1 Myth 1: Full control over the money supply

Contrary to popular belief, central banks do not unilaterally control the money supply. Modern money creation is endogenous, driven primarily by commercial bank lending responding to credit demand. The Bank of England [27] demonstrated that reserves are supplied to maintain interest rates rather than control lending, implying that monetary policy primarily guides interest rates, not aggregate money quantities.

5.2 Myth 2: Low interest rates guarantee growth

Interest-rate reductions encourage borrowing, but their efficacy is conditional on economic conditions. For instance, post-2008 QE in Japan and the Eurozone did not

Myth	Description	Empirical evidence/reality
Central banks fully control the money supply	Belief that central banks dictate all money creation	Money creation is largely endogenous; bank lending and demand deposits drive broad money [27]
Low interest rates guarantee growth	Assumes lower borrowing costs automatically boost economic activity	Prolonged low rates may create asset bubbles without sustainable growth [15]
Inflation targeting ensures total stability	Belief that price stability alone stabilizes the economy	Inflation targeting may ignore asset-price inflation or financial instability [28]
Monetary policy alone achieves full employment	Assumes the central bank can create jobs without structural reforms	Employment depends on labor market flexibility, productivity, and fiscal policy [7]
Central banks operate independently of politics	Assumes complete autonomy	Fiscal pressures and political considerations often constrain policy choices [13]

Table 4.
Common myths versus realities in monetary policy.

produce sustained output growth, despite near-zero or negative interest rates [15, 23]. Low rates over extended periods can misallocate capital, inflate asset prices, and create financial vulnerabilities.

5.3 Myth 3: Inflation targeting ensures stability

Inflation targeting is a widely adopted policy framework. However, controlling headline CPI does not preclude financial instability. The 2007–2008 crisis highlighted that central banks may overlook housing, credit, and asset-price booms when focusing narrowly on consumer-price inflation [28]. Emerging markets, such as India, experienced moderate inflation alongside volatile capital flows, underscoring the limits of CPI-focused targets [26].

5.4 Myth 4: Monetary policy alone can achieve full employment

Labor-market outcomes are influenced by structural factors, including productivity, regulatory frameworks, and skill mismatches. Monetary interventions can affect short-term demand but cannot address structural unemployment or supply-side rigidities [7]. Policy must be coordinated with fiscal, educational, and labor-market reforms.

5.5 Myth 5: Central banks are fully independent

Although legal independence reduces political interference, central banks operate within broader macroeconomic and fiscal constraints. Sovereign debt pressures in emerging economies, or the dollar-peg arrangements in GCC countries, limit discretionary monetary action. Empirical studies indicate that deviations from target rates often reflect political and fiscal considerations rather than policy errors [2, 13].

Constraint	Description	Observed Implications
Impossible trinity	Fixed exchange rate + open capital flows + monetary independence cannot coexist	GCC countries prioritize exchange-rate stability; domestic rate flexibility is limited [2]
Fiscal dominance	Large deficits limit central-bank autonomy	Emerging markets show persistent inflationary pressures despite rate hikes [14]
Global capital flows	Volatility in foreign investment affects domestic credit	Sudden inflows/outflows amplify inflation or liquidity shocks [8]
Structural rigidity	Labor market, financial system constraints	Weak transmission of policy to output/ employment [9]
Digitalization and fintech	CBDCs, mobile payments alter monetary mechanisms	May accelerate or bypass conventional transmission (BIS, 2021 [29])

Table 5.
Key monetary policy realities and constraints (BIS= Bank for International Settlement).

6. Realities and policy constraints

Empirical and theoretical studies highlight that monetary policy is constrained by structural, institutional, and global factors. **Table 5** summarizes key constraints and observed impacts.

6.1 Global and regional observations

Developed economies: policy lags, credibility, and zero-lower-bound conditions limit effectiveness.

Emerging markets: fiscal dominance, shallow financial markets, and capital volatility weaken transmission.

GCC region: dollar peg prioritizes exchange-rate stability; liquidity management via repo/certificate facilities dominates [2].

7. Case studies

7.1 Real-world policy interventions illustrate both efficacy and limitations

Case study: the United States Federal Reserve's Quantitative Easing (QE) Program, 2008–2015

The United States Federal Reserve's response to the 2008 global financial crisis represents a defining case of unconventional monetary policy and provides clear empirical evidence of how monetary interventions can stabilize financial systems during systemic distress. QE was the principal policy instrument employed between 2008 and 2015, designed to expand liquidity, lower long-term yields, and restore credit functioning in the aftermath of the housing and banking collapse.

7.2 Background and policy rationale

The US financial system faced unprecedented liquidity shortages following the subprime mortgage crisis. Conventional policy instruments, such as the federal

Country/ region	Policy approach	Outcomes	Notes
USA (2008–2015)	QE and forward guidance	Long-term yields ↓, equity markets ↑	Stimulated aggregate demand; limited direct effect on employment
Eurozone (2014–2020)	Negative rates, QE	Lending ↑, bank profits ↓, inflation modest	ECB constrained by multicountry targets
Japan (2013–2020)	Yield-curve control	Stable 10-year yields, weak GDP growth	Structural issues limit monetary transmission
India (2016–2023)	Inflation targeting	CPI stabilized at 4–5%; output volatile	Fiscal pressures occasionally limited autonomy
UAE/GCC	Liquidity operations under USD peg	Short-term stability	Interest-rate adjustments largely pass-through from US Fed

Table 6.
Selected central-bank case studies.

funds rate, had reached the zero lower bound by December 2008 (Bernanke, 2020 [30]). With limited room for traditional rate cuts, the Federal Reserve adopted large-scale asset purchases (LSAPs), targeting long-term treasury securities and mortgage-backed securities (MBS). The underlying rationale was that by purchasing these securities, the central bank (refer to **Table 6**) could lower long-term yields, reduce borrowing costs, and stimulate investment and consumption through portfolio rebalancing effects [24].

7.3 Implementation phases

QE was implemented in three distinct phases:

- QE1 (2008–2010): purchases of $1.75 trillion in treasury and agency securities.

- QE2 (2010–2011): purchases of $600 billion in treasury securities to counter deflationary pressures.

- QE3 (2012–2014): open-ended monthly purchases of $85 billion in treasury and MBS assets until tapering began in late 2014 [31].

The cumulative balance-sheet expansion exceeded $4.5 trillion by 2015, marking the most extensive liquidity intervention in US monetary history.

7.4 Empirical outcomes

Quantitative evaluations suggest that QE effectively reduced long-term yields by 80–120 basis points across maturities [32]. Event studies demonstrate immediate declines in Treasury and MBS yields following policy announcements, confirming market sensitivity to central-bank signaling.

Equity prices rose significantly, with the S&P 500 increasing by over 120% between March 2009 and December 2014, reflecting improved market sentiment and portfolio reallocation [33]. However, real-sector transmission remained moderate. While credit availability improved, the recovery in investment and employment was gradual due to lingering deleveraging in the private sector.

Inflation expectations stabilized around the Federal Reserve's implicit 2% target, indicating success in anchoring deflationary risks. Nonetheless, critics argued that the policy produced distributional side effects – particularly asset-price inflation that disproportionately benefited wealthier households and institutional investors [34].

7.5 Challenges and policy trade-offs

Three major challenges emerged:

1. Diminishing marginal returns: successive QE rounds generated smaller yield effects, suggesting declining efficiency of liquidity injections [15].

2. Exit strategy risks: Balance-sheet normalization introduced concerns about potential market disruptions once tapering began. The "taper tantrum" episode in mid-2013, triggered by indications of QE withdrawal, led to short-term bond yield spikes and capital outflows from emerging markets [35].

3. Global spillovers: QE-induced capital inflows into emerging markets caused currency appreciation and volatility, underscoring the interconnectedness of global monetary regimes (IMF, 2014 [36]).

7.6 Evaluation and lessons learned

Overall, the Federal Reserve's QE program met its short-term objectives: it restored market liquidity, reduced borrowing costs, and mitigated deflationary pressures. The absence of runaway inflation, despite aggressive money creation, supported the post-Keynesian argument that monetary expansion in liquidity-trap conditions does not necessarily trigger price instability [7].

However, the policy also highlighted key limitations. Monetary stimulus cannot substitute for structural or fiscal reforms when private-sector confidence and investment remain weak. The persistence of low productivity growth during the recovery years (2010–2015) suggests that liquidity alone was insufficient to generate sustainable output expansion.

Furthermore, the Fed's communication strategy, including forward guidance and transparency measures, proved critical in managing expectations. The success of QE depended as much on credibility and predictability as on the volume of asset purchases. This reinforces the broader principle that monetary policy effectiveness relies on trust and institutional reputation, not merely instrument deployment.

7.7 Implications for global and regional economies

The QE case carries implications for both advanced and emerging economies. Central banks in the Eurozone, Japan, and later emerging markets adopted variants of QE, reflecting its perceived effectiveness as a crisis-management tool. However, replication requires caution: in economies with underdeveloped financial systems or fixed exchange-rate regimes, LSAPs may produce destabilizing capital flows and inflationary pressures.

For the GCC countries, including the UAE, QE experiences demonstrate that while currency pegs limit conventional autonomy, alternative liquidity-management tools – such as repo facilities and certificate-of-deposit programs – can replicate some stabilizing effects without altering exchange-rate commitments [2].

7.8 Conclusion

The US QE experience underscores the dual nature of modern monetary policy: it is effective in averting financial collapse and stabilizing expectations, yet constrained in generating self-sustaining real growth. The case reaffirms that monetary interventions, when executed with credibility and coordination, are indispensable during crises but must be complemented by structural and fiscal measures to secure long-term recovery.

8. Future of monetary policy

Emerging trends indicate several shifts:

1. Digital currencies and fintech: CBDCs may accelerate payments and change liquidity management (BIS, 2021).

2. Macroprudential integration: central banks increasingly combine monetary policy with financial stability mandates.

3. Climate risk considerations: environmental factors are influencing asset purchases and collateral frameworks [37].

4. AI and big data analytics: real-time monitoring and predictive models improve forecasting but require careful validation [4].

Emerging trends indicate several shifts (refer to **Table 7**).

9. Conclusion

Monetary policy remains an essential instrument for macroeconomic stabilization, yet its effectiveness is neither uniform nor unconditional. While monetary authorities play a central role in managing inflation, liquidity, and short-

Trend	Mechanism	Implications
Digital currencies	Faster settlement, direct transmission	Alters bank's role in money creation
Macroprudential tools	Capital buffers, countercyclical measures	Reduces systemic risk
Climate integration	Green asset purchases	Aligns policy with sustainability goals
1 I analytics	High-frequency monitoring	Better forecasting; potential over-reliance

Table 7.
Emerging trends in monetary policy.

term economic fluctuations, the practical impact of their interventions is shaped by a complex interaction of institutional structures, market conditions, and global financial linkages. Established theoretical frameworks – ranging from monetarist and New Keynesian models to heterodox perspectives – offer structured guidance for policy formulation, but they do not fully account for the diversity of economic environments in which monetary policy operates. As a result, the translation of theoretical prescriptions into real-world outcomes depends heavily on country-specific institutional design, the credibility of central banks, and the degree of coordination with fiscal authorities.

Empirical evidence presented in this chapter demonstrates that monetary policy transmission varies significantly across regions and stages of economic development. In advanced economies, well-developed financial markets and credible policy frameworks allow interest rate changes and unconventional measures to influence expectations, asset prices, and credit conditions with relatively predictable effects. In contrast, emerging market economies often experience weaker and more volatile transmission due to structural constraints, capital flow sensitivity, and fiscal dominance, which limit the autonomy and effectiveness of central banks. In the case of GCC economies, exchange-rate pegs and open capital accounts further restrict independent monetary action, shifting the policy focus toward liquidity management and financial stability rather than active countercyclical intervention. These variations underscore that monetary policy cannot be assessed independently of broader economic and institutional contexts.

The chapter also highlights the persistence of misconceptions regarding the scope and capabilities of central banks. Monetary authorities are frequently perceived as possessing direct control over money creation, economic growth, and employment outcomes, despite substantial evidence that many of these processes are endogenous and influenced by private-sector behavior. Such misconceptions risk generating unrealistic expectations about what monetary policy can achieve, particularly in periods of economic stress. Clear communication, transparency, and well-defined policy mandates are therefore essential to maintaining credibility and preventing the misinterpretation of policy actions.

Looking forward, the evolving landscape of monetary policy reflects broader transformations in financial systems and economic priorities. The increasing relevance of digital payment systems and central bank digital currencies, the incorporation of climate-related risks into financial supervision, and the expanded use of macroprudential tools are likely to reshape policy frameworks in the coming years. These developments suggest a gradual shift from narrowly defined price-stability objectives toward a more integrated approach that recognizes financial stability, sustainability, and systemic risk as core policy concerns. In this environment, monetary policy should be understood as both a powerful stabilizing mechanism and a constrained instrument whose effectiveness depends on adaptability, institutional credibility, and coordination with complementary economic policies.

Acknowledgment

Author used Chat GPT (Open AI) for getting an idea of **Tables 5** and **6**.

Author details

Ashok Chopra[1*] and Anita Rani Chopra[2]

1 Amity University Dubai, Dubai, UAE

2 FIT Institute Dubai, Dubai, UAE

*Address all correspondence to: achopra@amityuniversity.ae

References

[1] Mishkin FS. The Economics of Money, Banking, and Financial Markets. 12th ed. Pearson; 2019

[2] IMF. United Arab Emirates: 2023 Article IV Consultation. International Monetary Fund; 2023

[3] Bernanke BS, Gertler M. Inside the black box: The credit channel of monetary policy transmission. Journal of Economic Perspectives. 1995;**9**(4):27–48

[4] Cecchetti SG, Schoenholtz KL. Money, Banking, and Financial Markets. 6th ed. McGraw-Hill; 2021

[5] Bernanke BS, Laubach T, Mishkin FS, Posen AS. Inflation Targeting: Lessons from the International Experience. Princeton University Press; 1999

[6] Svensson LEO. Inflation forecast targeting: Implementing and monitoring inflation targets. European Economic Review. 1997;**41**(6):1111–1146

[7] Blanchard O. On the future of macroeconomic models. Oxford Review of Economic Policy. 2018;**34**(1–2):43–54

[8] Borio C. Monetary policy frameworks in EMEs: Practice ahead of theory. BIS Papers. 2021;**118**

[9] Mishra P, Montiel P, Sengupta R. Monetary transmission in developing countries: Evidence and implications. IMF Economic Review. 2016;**64**(4):661–705

[10] Woodford M. Interest and Prices: Foundations of a Theory of Monetary Policy. Princeton University Press; 2003

[11] Christiano L, Eichenbaum M, Evans C. Monetary policy shocks: What have we learned and to what end? In Handbook of Macroeconomics. Vol. **1A**. Elsevier; 1999. p. 65–148

[12] Cukierman A, Web SB, Neyapti B. Measuring the independence of central banks and its effect on policy outcomes. The world bank economic review. 1992;**6**(3):353–398

[13] Reinhart CM, Rogoff KS. This Time Is Different: Eight Centuries of Financial Folly. Princeton University Press; 2011

[14] Sargent TJ, Wallace N. Some unpleasant monetarist arithmetic. Federal Reserve Bank of Minneapolis Quarterly Review. 1981;**5**(3):1–17

[15] Borio C, Disyatat P. Unconventional monetary policies: An appraisal. Manchester School. 2010;**78**(s1):53–89

[16] Lucas RE. Expectations and the neutrality of money. Journal of Economic Theory. 1972;**4**(2):103–124

[17] Mundell RA. Capital mobility and stabilization policy under fixed and flexible exchange rates. Canadian Journal of Economics and Political Science. 1963;**29**(4):475–485

[18] Blinder A, Ehrmann M, de Haan J, Jansen DJ. Necessity as the mother of invention: Monetary policy after the crisis. Economic Policy. 2017;**32**(92):707–755

[19] Friedman M. The role of monetary policy. American Economic Review. 1968;**58**(1):1–17

[20] Bernanke B, Mishkin F. Central bank behavior and the strategy of monetary policy: observations from six industrialized countries. NBER Macroeconomics Annual. 1992;7:183–228

[21] Clarida R, Galí J, Gertler M. The science of monetary policy: A New Keynesian perspective. Journal of Economic Literature. 1999;**37**(4):1661–1707

[22] Keynes JM. The General Theory of Employment, Interest and Money. Macmillan; 1936

[23] Hattori M, Yetman J. The evolution of yield curve control: Bank of [15] Japan's experience. BIS Quarterly Review. 2020

[24] Gagnon J, Raskin M, Remache J, Sack B. The financial market effects of the Federal Reserve's large-scale asset purchases. International Journal of Central Banking. 2011;**7**(1):3–43

[25] Rostagno M, Altavilla C, Carboni G, Lemke W, Motto R, Saint Guilhem A, Yiangou J (2019). A tale of two decades: The ECB's monetary policy at 20. ECB Occasional Paper Series, No. 234

[26] Patra MD, Kapur M (2012). A monetary policy model without money for India. IMF Working Paper No. 12/91

[27] McLeay M, Radia A, Thomas R. Money creation in the modern economy. Bank of England Quarterly Bulletin. 2014;**54**(1):14–27

[28] Frankel J (2012). Inflation targeting is dead: Long live nominal GDP targeting. World Bank Policy Research Working Paper No. 5826

[29] Bank for International Settlements. Central bank digital currencies: System design and interoperability. Bank for International Settlements. 2021. https://www.bis.org/publ/othp33.htm

[30] Bernanke BS. The new tools of monetary policy. American Economic Review. 2020;**110**(4):943–983

[31] Federal Reserve Board. Monetary Policy Report to the Congress. Washington, DC; 2014

[32] Krishnamurthy A, Vissing-Jorgensen A. The effects of quantitative easing on interest rates: Channels and implications for policy. Brookings Papers on Economic Activity. 2011;**2011**(2):215–287

[33] Joyce M, Lasaosa A, Stevens I, Tong M. The financial market impact of quantitative easing in the United Kingdom. International Journal of Central Banking. 2012;**8**(3):113–161

[34] Coibion O, Gorodnichenko Y, Kueng L, Silvia J. Innocent bystanders? Monetary policy and inequality. Journal of Monetary Economics. 2017;**88**:70–89

[35] Neely CJ. Unconventional monetary policy had large international effects. Journal of Banking & Finance. 2015;**52**:101–111

[36] International Monetary Fund. Research Dept. World Economic Outlook, April: Recovery Strengthens, Remains Uneven. International Monetary. International Monetary Fund. 2014

[37] NGFS. Guide for Integrating Climate-related Risks into Central Bank Operations. Network for Greening the Financial System; 2020

Chapter 3

The Myth of Decentralized Money: Can Cryptocurrencies Replace Central Bank Monetary Policy?

Basma Almisshal

Abstract

The advent of decentralized cryptocurrencies has reignited fundamental debates in monetary economics about the nature and future of money. Proponents of digital currencies argue that decentralized, algorithmically governed assets can supplant central banks in managing monetary conditions and stabilizing economic outcomes. This chapter critically examines this proposition by evaluating cryptocurrencies against the classical functions of money and the core instruments of monetary policy. Grounded in monetary theory – from Friedman's monetarism and Mises' Austrian framework to Modern Monetary Theory – and extended through a behavioral finance lens, the analysis reveals that widespread belief in cryptocurrency as a viable monetary policy alternative is driven not merely by technological innovation but by deeply embedded cognitive biases, including overconfidence, narrative-driven speculation, and institutional distrust. The chapter also treats money as an economic asset subject to market competition. Drawing on Austrian economic theory and classical competition principles, the analysis evaluates whether decentralized currencies can realistically compete with sovereign money in an open monetary market. By integrating monetary economics with strategic competition frameworks, the chapter explores whether cryptocurrencies can achieve monetary dominance through efficiency, cost advantages, or differentiated value propositions. Based on principles from strategic business theories such as differentiation and cost-leadership, the chapter treats money as a competitive good subject to market dynamics, ultimately concluding that while cryptocurrencies represent a significant financial innovation, they fundamentally lack the institutional architecture and behavioral predictability required to replace central bank monetary policy.

Keywords: cryptocurrency, monetary policy, behavioral finance, decentralized finance, central banking, Bitcoin, CBDC, free-market money, financial innovation

1. Introduction

The emergence of Bitcoin in 2009, followed by thousands of alternative cryptocurrencies and the rise of decentralized finance (DeFi), has prompted a fundamental rethinking of monetary systems globally. At the heart of this debate lies a provocative question: can decentralized digital currencies replace the monetary policy apparatus of central banks? This chapter addresses that question directly, situating it within classical and contemporary monetary theory while incorporating insights from behavioral finance and competitive market dynamics.

Monetary policy – encompassing interest rate decisions, money supply management, inflation targeting, and financial stability oversight – has been the domain of central banks for over a century. Institutions such as the U.S. Federal Reserve, the European Central Bank, and the Bank of England operate under mandates that require nuanced, discretionary responses to complex macroeconomic conditions. The algorithmic determinism of Bitcoin, with its fixed supply cap of 21 million units, signals a shift in monetary governance from institutional discretion toward rule-based execution embedded in code.

The appeal of decentralized money is not merely technical – it is deeply behavioral. The 2008 global financial crisis exposed the fragility of centralized financial systems and triggered widespread institutional distrust, a context within which Bitcoin subsequently emerged as an alternative monetary paradigm [1, 2]. Bitcoin emerged at precisely this moment, offering an alternative monetary narrative free from institutional capture, inflationary manipulation, and political interference. This narrative has proven extraordinarily powerful, attracting trillions of dollars in capital and spawning an entire ecosystem of digital financial innovation.

Yet, the gap between the narrative of decentralized money and the reality of its monetary function remains substantial. This chapter argues that cryptocurrencies, while representing a genuine and important financial innovation, do not – and structurally cannot – replace the monetary policy functions of central banks. The myth of decentralized money is not merely a technical misunderstanding; it reflects behavioral biases, competitive market positioning, and the enduring human desire for monetary alternatives during episodes of institutional crisis.

The chapter is organized as follows: Section 2 reviews monetary theory and the functions of money. Section 3 examines cryptocurrencies as a competitive monetary good through the lens of market competition and strategic differentiation. Section 4 evaluates the monetary policy limitations of cryptocurrencies. Section 5 analyzes the behavioral finance dimensions of crypto adoption. Section 6 assesses the prospects for Central Bank Digital Currencies (CBDCs). Section 7 discusses the free-market monetary order perspective. Section 8 presents the conclusion.

2. Monetary theory and the functions of money

From a technological and economic perspective, cryptocurrencies represent a novel form of digital asset built on distributed ledger technology. As outlined by Narayanan et al. [3], Bitcoin combines cryptographic verification with decentralized consensus mechanisms to enable trustless transactions without a central authority. Similarly, Böhme et al. [4] describe Bitcoin as a socio-technical system that brings together economic incentives, cryptography, and governance structures. These features distinguish cryptocurrencies from both traditional forms of money and conventional financial assets.

2.1 Classical functions of money

The classical definition of money identifies three core functions: a medium of exchange, a store of value, and a unit of account [5]. A medium of exchange eliminates the inefficiencies of barter by providing a commonly accepted intermediary good. A store of value enables the deferral of purchasing power through time. A unit of account provides a standardized measure for pricing goods and services across an economy.

For any asset to function as money in a macroeconomically meaningful sense, it must fulfill all three functions reliably and simultaneously [5]. Bitcoin has demonstrated limited success as a medium of exchange due to transaction cost volatility, throughput limitations, and price instability. Its function as a store of value remains contested, given extreme price volatility – a 70–80% drawdown in market value occurred in both 2018 and 2022 [6]. Its role as a unit of account remains minimal, with virtually no goods and services priced natively in Bitcoin.

2.2 Monetarist perspective

Milton Friedman's monetarism establishes a direct relationship between money supply growth and inflation, captured in the quantity theory of money: $MV = PQ$, where M is the money supply, V is the velocity of circulation, P is the price level, and Q is the real output [7]. Friedman advocated greater reliance on predictable, rule-based management of money supply growth over discretionary political interference. In this sense, Bitcoin's fixed supply might appear aligned with monetarist principles – it is, by design, deflationary and rule-governed.

However, Friedman's framework assumes a relatively stable velocity of money and a functioning payments system. Bitcoin's velocity is highly unstable, its use as a medium of exchange is limited, and its price volatility undermines any predictable relationship between supply and price levels. Thus, while Bitcoin superficially resembles a Friedmanian money supply rule, it lacks the systemic embedding required for effective macroeconomic management [7].

2.3 Austrian school perspectives

The Austrian school, represented most prominently by Ludwig von Mises and Murray Rothbard, offers perhaps the most philosophically sympathetic theoretical grounding for cryptocurrencies [8]. Mises' regression theorem holds that money must be traceable to a prior commodity value – a criterion that Bitcoin's proponents argue, controversially, is satisfied by its computational scarcity and proof-of-work energy expenditure, though Mises himself wrote before the existence of digital assets and made no such claim. Rothbard's advocacy for free banking and commodity-backed money aligns with Bitcoin's rejection of the central bank monopoly on money creation.

More broadly, Austrian business cycle theory attributes boom–bust cycles to artificial credit expansion by central banks and fractional-reserve banking. From this perspective, decentralized money that cannot be inflated appears as a structural remedy rather than a mere alternative. Treating money as a competitive good, shaped by competition, differentiation, and cost leadership, is rooted in the Austrian tradition.

Austrian monetary theory views money as an emergent market institution rather than a state-designed mechanism. Carl Menger's theory of the origin of money argues that money arises spontaneously through market exchange as individuals gradually converge on the most marketable commodity. Historically, commodities such as gold and silver acquired monetary status because they possessed superior characteristics – durability, divisibility, portability, and scarcity – relative to alternative goods. From this perspective, cryptocurrencies represent a modern technological attempt to replicate these properties through algorithmic scarcity and cryptographic verification rather than physical scarcity.

Friedrich Hayek later extended this reasoning by proposing that monetary competition among privately issued currencies would discipline issuers and improve monetary quality. Under a competitive monetary system, currencies that maintain purchasing power stability and transactional efficiency would attract users, while poorly managed currencies would lose market share. Cryptocurrencies, therefore, represent a partial realization of Hayek's proposal for competing currencies, although they differ from Hayek's original framework in that their issuance is algorithmic rather than institutionally managed.

2.4 Modern monetary theory

In sharp contrast, Modern Monetary Theory (MMT) holds that governments which issue their own currency are not revenue-constrained in the conventional sense – they can issue currency to meet obligations, with inflation serving as the operative constraint rather than fiscal solvency [9]. From an MMT standpoint, cryptocurrencies cannot serve the monetary policy function precisely because they lack the institutional backing and fiscal coordination that give fiat money its systemic power. Decentralized money, in this view, is not an alternative monetary system; it is a privately issued asset that operates entirely outside the sovereign monetary framework.

3. Money as a competitive good: Competition, differentiation, and market dynamics

3.1 The law of competition and monetary evolution

The law of competition – a foundational principle in classical and neoclassical economics – holds that in free markets, competing suppliers will drive prices toward the costs of production, and consumers will gravitate toward the most efficient providers [10]. Applied to money, this principle suggests that if multiple monetary instruments compete, the most efficient and most trusted money will tend to displace inferior alternatives over time. In a monetary economy, competition between currencies operates through several mechanisms: institutional credibility, transaction efficiency, purchasing power stability, and network adoption. Unlike conventional goods, however, money exhibits strong network externalities. The usefulness of a currency increases with the number of individuals who accept it, creating significant barriers to entry for new monetary competitors. As a result, even if a technologically superior currency emerges, the displacement of the incumbent currency may occur slowly or remain limited to niche markets. This network dynamic explains why historically dominant currencies, such as the US dollar, maintain global monetary influence despite the existence of alternative financial technologies.

Cryptocurrency advocates implicitly invoke this logic: if Bitcoin is superior to fiat money in terms of predictability, security, and resistance to debasement, market competition should eventually favor its adoption. This argument draws on Friedrich Hayek's denationalization of money thesis, which proposed that competing private currencies would discipline monetary issuers and produce superior monetary outcomes compared to state monopolies [11]. However, the competitive monetary landscape is more complex: fiat money, with institutional backing, benefits from enormous incumbency advantages – deep liquidity, universal acceptance, and sovereign legitimacy – that cryptocurrencies have thus far been unable to overcome.

This competitive dynamic can be further examined through Porter's Five Forces framework, which offers a structured lens for analyzing competitive pressures within an industry [12, 13]. In the monetary context, the threat of new entrants (cryptocurrencies), the bargaining power of users (currency holders), the threat of substitutes (alternative digital assets and payment systems), and rivalry among existing monetary systems play a role in shaping how money evolves as a competitive good. Unlike traditional industries, however, the bargaining power of suppliers is effectively embedded within institutional frameworks, as central banks maintain control over monetary issuance and policy tools. This asymmetry reinforces the structural advantage of sovereign money despite technological disruption.

3.2 Differentiation strategy and crypto's value proposition

In Porter's framework of competitive strategy [14], a differentiation strategy involves creating a product perceived as unique along dimensions that consumers value, allowing for a premium market position. Cryptocurrencies have pursued an aggressive differentiation strategy relative to fiat money: decentralization (resistance to censorship and confiscation), scarcity (Bitcoin's fixed supply), and programmability (smart contracts in Ethereum and DeFi ecosystems).

This differentiation has been remarkably successful in capturing a specific market segment – technologically sophisticated investors, libertarian-leaning communities, residents of high-inflation economies, and institutional investors seeking uncorrelated assets. However, differentiation in the monetary context encounters a fundamental paradox: the more a monetary asset differentiates itself from the properties of universally accepted money, the less it can function as money in practice. This reflects Porter's argument on competitive positioning [13], which states that differentiation must align with core consumer needs; in monetary systems, those needs are monetary stability and broad public acceptance rather than uniqueness.

3.3 Cost-leadership and stablecoins

The cost-leadership strategic paradigm – achieving the lowest cost of provision to capture market share – finds its clearest monetary analog in stablecoins such as USDT and USDC, which offer the digital efficiency of crypto with the price stability of fiat [15]. Stablecoins reduce the transactional cost of international remittances, cross-border payments, and DeFi participation, offering a lower-cost payment

Criterion	Fiat money	Bitcoin	Stablecoins	CBDC
Medium of exchange	High	Low	Medium	High
Store of value	Medium	Speculative	Stable (pegged)	High
Unit of account	High	Low	Medium	High
Inflation control	Central bank	Algorithmic cap	Peg-based	CB-managed
Lender of last resort	Yes	No	No	Possible
Legal tender status	Yes	Rarely	No	Yes
Programmability	Limited	Limited	High	High
Regulatory oversight	Full	Minimal	Emerging	Full

Source: Author's compilation based on monetary economics literature.

Table 1.
Comparative assessment of monetary instruments across key criteria.

mechanism than traditional correspondent banking. Economically, blockchain-based systems reduce transaction and verification costs, with implications for the structure of financial intermediation [16]. However, these efficiencies do not extend to monetary policy functions, which remain dependent on institutional credibility and macroeconomic coordination. From a strategic management perspective, stablecoins represent a hybrid competitive strategy combining elements of cost leadership and technological differentiation. By leveraging blockchain infrastructure, stablecoin issuers significantly reduce settlement time and transaction costs relative to traditional cross-border banking systems. However, their value proposition remains fundamentally dependent on the credibility of the underlying fiat currency reserves. This creates a strategic asymmetry: while stablecoins can compete in payment efficiency, they cannot independently compete in monetary policy credibility, which remains anchored in sovereign institutions.

However, cost-leadership in payments does not translate to monetary policy capability. Stablecoins are pegged to fiat currencies – they are derivative monetary instruments whose value and stability depend entirely on the underlying fiat monetary system they claim to challenge. In this sense, stablecoins illustrate a strategic positioning that partially converges toward the core value proposition of fiat money rather than displacing it, in line with Porter's framework [13], where hybrid strategies often depend on the structure of the dominant industry. Their systemic resilience depends on the quality of their reserve management, as the collapse of the TerraUSD stablecoin in May 2022 demonstrated, with the estimated destruction of approximately $40 billion in market capitalization within days [6, 17]. **Table 1** summarizes the comparative characteristics of fiat money, Bitcoin, stablecoins, and CBDCs across major monetary criteria.

3.4 Porter's five forces and the structure of monetary competition

Applying Porter's Five Forces to monetary systems provides a structured lens through which the competitive dynamics between cryptocurrencies and sovereign money can be systematically examined [12, 13]. In this framework, industry structure is shaped by five fundamental forces: the threat of new entrants, the bargaining power of buyers, the bargaining power of suppliers, the threat of substitute products or services, and the intensity of rivalry among existing competitors.

Within cryptocurrency markets, the threat of new entrants is relatively high. The technological requirements for creating new tokens are limited, and barriers to entry remain comparatively low. As a result, the market has experienced a rapid proliferation of cryptocurrencies, the majority of which fail to achieve sustained adoption or long-term credibility.

The bargaining power of buyers, in this context represented by monetary users, is also significant. Users can, in principle, switch between different monetary instruments with relatively low direct costs. However, this apparent flexibility is constrained by strong network effects, which reinforce the dominance of widely accepted currencies such as the US dollar and limit the practical substitutability of alternative forms of money.

The bargaining power of suppliers can be interpreted through the institutional role of central banks and monetary authorities. These entities influence the supply, stability, and regulatory environment of fiat currencies, thereby shaping the broader competitive landscape. Their policy tools and legal authority contribute to sustaining confidence in sovereign money and reinforcing its position within the monetary system.

The threat of substitute products or services is substantial. Cryptocurrencies do not compete solely with fiat currencies but also with a growing range of alternatives, including stablecoins, digital payment platforms, and emerging central bank digital currencies (CBDCs). Each of these instruments offers different combinations of stability, efficiency, and trust, intensifying substitution pressures.

Finally, the intensity of rivalry among existing competitors within the cryptocurrency ecosystem is high. The market is characterized by fragmentation, rapid innovation, and speculative dynamics, with numerous projects competing for user adoption, liquidity, and technological relevance.

Taken together, these five forces indicate that cryptocurrencies operate within a highly competitive and structurally constrained environment. Despite their technological innovation, they lack the institutional reinforcement, regulatory backing, and network dominance that underpin the stability and widespread acceptance of sovereign money [14].

4. Evaluating cryptocurrency as a monetary policy instrument

4.1 The absence of monetary policy mechanisms

Central bank monetary policy operates through a sophisticated toolkit: open market operations, reserve requirements, policy interest rates, forward guidance, and emergency liquidity facilities. These instruments enable central banks to respond dynamically to cyclical fluctuations, financial crises, deflationary traps, and external shocks. The 2008–2009 global financial crisis and the 2020 COVID-19 pandemic both demonstrated the critical importance of discretionary monetary intervention in preventing systemic collapse [2].

Bitcoin and most cryptocurrencies possess none of these policy instruments. Supply is algorithmically predetermined, and there is no issuing authority capable of expanding liquidity in response to systemic stress. The absence of a lender-of-last-resort function has serious consequences: during periods of financial panic, the ability of central banks to provide unlimited liquidity to solvent but illiquid institutions is the primary mechanism preventing bank runs from cascading into systemic crises. DeFi protocols, which operate through smart contracts, offer no equivalent mechanism.

4.2 Deflationary dynamics

Bitcoin's fixed supply creates a structurally deflationary monetary environment as economic output grows relative to the monetary supply. Classical and Keynesian economics both identify deflation as potentially destabilizing: falling prices incentivize the deferral of consumption and investment, creating deflationary spirals that depress output and employment [18]. Japan's "lost decade" and the Great Depression are historical illustrations of how deflationary monetary conditions impede economic recovery.

Austrian economists challenge this analysis, arguing that in a free market, mild deflation driven by productivity gains is benign and that central bank-induced inflation is the greater harm. While this perspective has theoretical coherence, it remains empirically contested. Evidence from cryptocurrency markets indicates that Bitcoin's scarcity does not produce the gradual, productivity-linked deflation of Austrian theory – instead, it generates extreme speculative volatility driven by demand dynamics and market sentiment. Empirical research consistently demonstrates that Bitcoin operates predominantly as a speculative asset rather than a monetary base. Baur, Hong, and Lee [19] find that Bitcoin is held primarily for speculative purposes, with its return dynamics largely decoupled from any conventional monetary function. Corbet et al. [20] further document that cryptocurrency liquidity and volatility interact in mutually reinforcing ways that are fundamentally incompatible with the stability required of a monetary standard. Price movements are driven overwhelmingly by investor sentiment, liquidity conditions, and speculative trading cycles rather than macroeconomic fundamentals. As a result, the deflationary narrative associated with a fixed supply does not translate into price stability, which is the critical prerequisite for a functioning monetary standard.

The dynamics of cryptocurrency adoption can also be interpreted through the lens of tokenomics. Cong et al. [21] show that the value and adoption of digital tokens are driven by network growth, incentives, and user expectations rather than primarily by intrinsic monetary utility. This reinforces the argument that cryptocurrencies derive value from speculative and coordination dynamics rather than from fulfilling traditional monetary functions.

4.3 Volatility as a disqualifying property

Price volatility is perhaps the single most significant barrier to cryptocurrency serving as a monetary policy anchor. Bitcoin's annualized volatility has consistently exceeded 70–80% in recent years, compared to approximately 15–20% for equity indices and less than 5% for major fiat currencies, as illustrated in **Figure 1**, which presents the rolling 30-day annualized volatility of Bitcoin, gold, and the S&P 500 from 2013 to 2025. A monetary system built on an asset of such volatility cannot perform the unit-of-account and store-of-value functions required for macroeconomic stability [16]. **Table 2** presents the structural limitations of cryptocurrencies when evaluated against conventional monetary policy instruments.

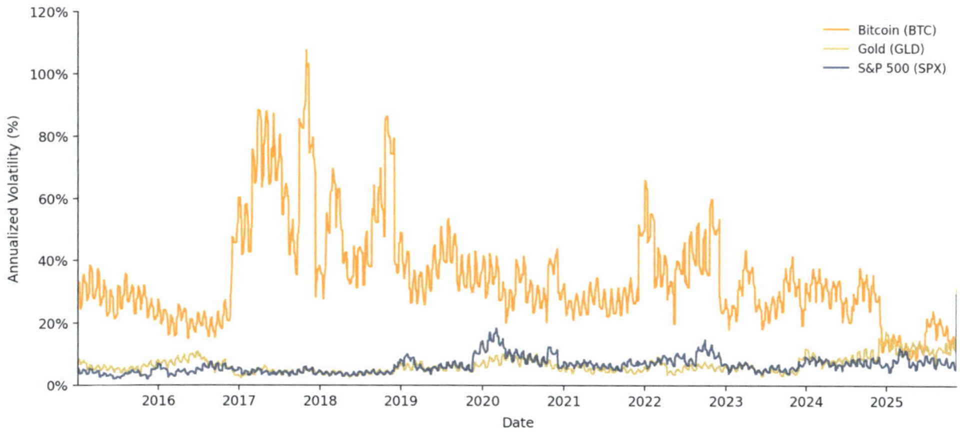

Figure 1.
Rolling 30-day annualized volatility: Bitcoin, gold, and S&P 500 (2015–2025). Source: Author's calculations based on historical daily price data retrieved from Investing.com historical data series for Bitcoin, Gold Futures, and the S&P 500 Index [22].

Monetary policy tool	Central bank mechanism	Crypto equivalent	Effectiveness
Interest rate setting	Policy rate adjustments	None (fixed supply)	Absent
Quantitative easing	Asset purchases	Mining rewards (diminishing)	Absent
Reserve requirements	Minimum bank reserves	None	Absent
Open market operations	Buy/sell gov. securities	None	Absent
Exchange rate management	FX interventions	Market-determined only	Absent
Lender of last resort	Emergency liquidity	No equivalent	Absent
Inflation targeting	Rate policy + guidance	Fixed supply cap (BTC)	Partial/ Deflationary

Source: Author's compilation based on monetary economics literature.

Table 2.
Cryptocurrency limitations as monetary policy instruments.

5. Behavioral finance dimensions of cryptocurrency adoption

5.1 The behavioral architecture of the crypto narrative

Behavioral finance, pioneered by Kahneman and Tversky through prospect theory, identifies systematic cognitive biases that cause economic agents to deviate from rational utility maximization [23]. These biases are not incidental to cryptocurrency markets – they are constitutive of them. The extraordinary valuations achieved by Bitcoin and other cryptocurrencies cannot be explained by fundamental monetary utility; they are, in large part, products of behavioral dynamics. In this context, cryptocurrencies resemble historical episodes of financial innovation, where technological promise interacts with speculative psychology. Similar dynamics were observed during the dot-com bubble, where technological narratives about the internet produced valuation levels disconnected from near-term economic fundamentals. The persistence of the cryptocurrency narrative illustrates how technological legitimacy can amplify behavioral biases in financial markets.

Robert Shiller's concept of narrative economics holds that economic behavior is driven by the viral spread of compelling narratives that capture the imagination and activate social contagion [24]. The Bitcoin narrative – decentralized, scarce, anti-establishment, technologically sovereign – is one of the most powerful economic narratives of the early twenty-first century. It has proven capable of sustaining investor commitment through multiple 70–80% drawdowns, a feat that no fundamental monetary function could justify.

5.2 Key behavioral biases in cryptocurrency markets

Several behavioral biases are particularly prominent in interpreting the dynamics of cryptocurrency adoption. Overconfidence bias leads investors to systematically overestimate their ability to predict and profit from cryptocurrency price movements, fueling speculative bubbles. Herding behavior – the tendency to follow crowd actions rather than independent analysis – amplifies price momentum in both directions, producing the characteristic boom-bust cycles observed in crypto markets [21]. Empirical decomposition of investor sentiment in cryptocurrency markets confirms this dual dynamic: Almisshal and Bulut [25] demonstrate that irrational sentiment – driven by heuristic overreaction and emotional contagion – generates short-lived but pronounced volatility spikes, while rational, information-based sentiment produces more gradual and persistent effects on returns. This behavioral decomposition provides granular evidence that it is precisely the speculative, emotionally driven component of investor sentiment that destabilizes cryptocurrency markets, rather than informed price discovery.

The availability heuristic causes investors to weigh recent high returns disproportionately in forming expectations about future performance, sustaining

Behavioral bias	Description	Effect on crypto adoption
Overconfidence bias	Overestimation of ability to predict crypto returns	Drives speculative bubbles and inflated valuations
Narrative economics	Compelling stories (e.g., "digital gold") shape behavior	Sustains belief in crypto as monetary replacement
Institutional distrust	Post-2008 skepticism of banks and governments	Motivates flight to decentralized alternatives
Herding behavior	Investors follow crowd rather than fundamentals	Amplifies volatility and FOMO-driven cycles
Loss aversion	Fear of missing gains outweighs risk concerns	Sustains participation despite extreme volatility
Availability heuristic	Recent high returns shape probability estimates	Leads to unrealistic return expectations

Table 3.
Behavioral biases driving cryptocurrency adoption.

participation through periods of extreme risk. Loss aversion can intensify commitment to positions – the fear of realizing a loss leads holders to maintain positions well beyond rational exit points, known colloquially as "HODLing" in cryptocurrency communities. Institutional distrust, which surged following the 2008 financial crisis, provides the foundational behavioral motivation for decentralized money [2]. **Table 3** summarizes the major behavioral biases associated with cryptocurrency adoption and speculative participation.

5.3 Implications for monetary policy credibility

The behavioral dimensions of cryptocurrency markets have direct implications for monetary policy. Central bank credibility – the cornerstone of effective inflation management – depends on the public's belief that the central bank will maintain its mandate regardless of short-term political pressures [26]. The rise of cryptocurrencies as an alternative monetary narrative represents a form of credibility challenge: it signals that a significant portion of the population has lost confidence in institutional monetary management.

Central banks cannot dismiss this behavioral signal. The fact that millions of individuals globally have voluntarily adopted highly volatile, functionally limited digital assets as alternatives to stable fiat money is, in itself, macroeconomically significant. It reflects underlying institutional failures – real or perceived – that monetary authorities must address through better communication, transparency, and policy credibility.

6. Central bank digital currencies: Institutional response to the crypto challenge

6.1 The CBDC proposition

Central Bank Digital Currencies (CBDCs) represent the most important institutional response to the cryptocurrency challenge. A CBDC is a digital form of sovereign currency – a direct liability of the central bank, equivalent in status to physical banknotes but in digital form [27]. As of 2024, over 130 countries, representing more than 98% of global GDP, were in various stages of CBDC exploration, development, or deployment [28].

CBDCs offer a synthesis of the technological efficiencies of cryptocurrencies – programmability, instant settlement, reduced transaction costs – with the institutional stability and monetary policy functionality of central bank money. They represent, in Porter's strategic terms, a competitive response strategy: the incumbent monetary authority adopting the differentiating features of the challenger without surrendering its core competitive advantages.

6.2 CBDCs and monetary policy enhancement

Beyond payment efficiency, CBDCs offer potential enhancements to monetary policy transmission. Programmable CBDCs could, in principle, implement negative interest rates directly on digital cash holdings, bypassing the zero lower bound constraint that has limited conventional monetary policy since the 2008 crisis [29].

They could also enable targeted fiscal transfers with a precision impossible through conventional banking channels.

However, CBDCs also introduce significant risks. Disintermediation of commercial banks – if the public holds CBDC directly with the central bank rather than in commercial bank deposits – could undermine the credit creation mechanism that drives economic growth. Privacy concerns, the potential for real-time financial surveillance by governments, and cybersecurity vulnerabilities represent additional policy challenges that no major central bank has fully resolved.

6.3 Competitive dynamics between CBDCs and cryptocurrencies

The competitive relationship between CBDCs and decentralized cryptocurrencies illuminates broader monetary competition dynamics. CBDCs and Bitcoin are not substitutes – they serve fundamentally different functions and appeal to different market segments. Bitcoin appeals to those who prioritize censorship-resistance, privacy, and freedom from institutional oversight. CBDCs appeal to those who value stability, legal recognition, and seamless integration with the financial system. This segmentation suggests that the future monetary landscape will be pluralistic: sovereign digital money and private digital assets coexisting in a competitive ecosystem, with relative market share determined by regulatory frameworks, technological development, macroeconomic stability, and shifting consumer preferences.

7. The free market monetary order: Does competition vindicate decentralized money?

7.1 Hayek's denationalization thesis revisited

Friedrich Hayek's 1976 proposal for the denationalization of money argued that competing private currencies, freed from state monopoly, would produce superior monetary outcomes through market discipline [11]. Currency issuers would be constrained by competitive pressures to maintain the stability and utility of their monetary products; those who inflated or mismanaged their currencies would be punished by consumer exit.

Cryptocurrencies are, in a meaningful sense, the first large-scale empirical test of Hayek's proposition. However, the cryptocurrency experience also reveals the limitations of pure monetary competition. Hayek envisioned competing currencies issued by private institutions that would actively manage their supply in order to maintain stable purchasing power. Cryptocurrencies, by contrast, rely on rigid algorithmic supply rules that cannot respond to changing macroeconomic conditions. This distinction is critical: Hayek's proposal emphasized market discipline over discretionary policy, but it did not eliminate monetary management entirely. The cryptocurrency model, therefore, represents a more radical form of monetary decentralization than Hayek himself proposed. The result is instructive: the most successful cryptocurrency, Bitcoin, has not converged toward monetary stability – it has converged toward speculative investment behavior. Market competition has produced thousands of competing tokens, most of which have zero monetary utility, and a handful of liquid assets that function primarily as speculative instruments rather than as money.

7.2 Market failures in monetary competition

The failure of cryptocurrency markets to produce Hayekian monetary outcomes reflects fundamental market failures in monetary competition. Money is a coordination good: its value derives not from its intrinsic properties but from the network of users who accept it [30]. This network externality creates powerful incumbency advantages that make the displacement of established monetary systems extremely difficult, even by technically superior alternatives.

Moreover, monetary stability is a public good: it benefits all participants in an economy, regardless of whether they individually contribute to maintaining it. Public goods, in standard economic theory, are subject to underprovision by markets and require institutional provision. The free-market monetary order envisioned by Hayek and Rothbard may, therefore, be theoretically coherent but practically unachievable without an institutional anchor.

7.3 When free markets support decentralized money

There are, however, contexts in which free-market monetary dynamics do favor decentralized alternatives. In countries experiencing hyperinflation – Venezuela, Zimbabwe, Argentina – cryptocurrencies have served as genuine monetary substitutes, enabling citizens to preserve purchasing power in the absence of credible sovereign money [31]. Empirical evidence from these economies documents measurable increases in cryptocurrency adoption correlated with currency depreciation and capital controls, consistent with the theoretical prediction that a more stable monetary instrument will displace a failing one [4].

This suggests that the competitiveness of decentralized money is contextually determined by the quality of the incumbent monetary system. Where central bank monetary policy is credible and effective, decentralized alternatives occupy a complementary niche. Where it has failed, they can perform genuine monetary functions. This nuanced conclusion resists both the utopian claims of crypto maximalists and the dismissive skepticism of traditional monetary economists.

7.4 Monetary competition in the digital era

The emergence of cryptocurrencies, stablecoins, and CBDCs suggests that the global monetary system is entering a new phase of competitive coexistence. Rather than a binary choice between decentralized and sovereign money, the digital era may produce a layered monetary architecture in which different forms of money serve specialized functions. Cryptocurrencies may function primarily as speculative assets or stores of value for specific communities, stablecoins as payment infrastructure for digital markets, and CBDCs as sovereign digital settlement systems integrated with national monetary policy frameworks.

8. Conclusion

This chapter has examined the proposition that cryptocurrencies can replace central bank monetary policy through multiple theoretical lenses: classical monetary functions, monetarist theory, the Austrian school, competitive market dynamics, and behavioral finance. The conclusion demonstrates that cryptocurrencies represent a significant and enduring financial innovation, but they fundamentally lack the institutional architecture, policy flexibility, and behavioral stability required to replace central bank monetary policy in advanced economies.

The concept of decentralized money is considered a myth not because digital currencies lack value, but because the case for their monetary supremacy rests more on behavioral narrative than on functional monetary analysis. Overconfidence, institutional distrust, narrative economics, and herding behavior have produced valuations and adoption rates that far exceed what cryptocurrency's monetary utility can justify. These behavioral signals, nonetheless, carry important information for monetary authorities: they reflect genuine institutional deficits in transparency, credibility, and inclusivity that central banks must urgently address.

Treating money as any other competitive good – subject to the laws of competition, differentiation, cost-leadership, and consumer preference – reveals a pluralistic monetary future rather than a zero-sum displacement contest. CBDCs, stablecoins, and decentralized cryptocurrencies will likely coexist in a competitive digital monetary ecosystem, each serving distinct market segments and functional needs. The free market does work in monetary competition – but it works toward segmentation and coexistence, not toward the elimination of institutional money. Nevertheless, cryptocurrencies have demonstrated meaningful utility in areas such as cross-border payments, financial inclusion, and monetary substitution within economies experiencing monetary instability.

For policymakers, the appropriate response to the cryptocurrency challenge is not prohibition or dismissal but institutional adaptation. Central banks that succeed in combining the stability and policy functionality of sovereign money with the technological efficiency and transparency of digital systems will retain monetary dominance. Future research would benefit from empirically examining monetary substitution dynamics in high-inflation economies, where cryptocurrency adoption has been most significant, and from assessing the behavioral determinants of CBDC adoption relative to both fiat and decentralized alternatives.

AI tools disclosure

AI-assisted tools were used exclusively for language refinement, structural organization, and formatting support. All intellectual content, analysis, argumentation, and scholarly interpretation are the original work of the author. The author takes full responsibility for the accuracy and integrity of all content presented.

Author details

Basma Almisshal
Duzce University, Duzce, Turkey

*Address all correspondence to: basmahalmisshal@duzce.edu.tr

References

[1] Nakamoto S. Bitcoin: A Peer-to-Peer Electronic Cash System. 2008. Available from: https://bitcoin.org/bitcoin.pdf [Accessed: 2026-March-12]

[2] Bernanke BS. The Federal Reserve and the Financial Crisis. Princeton: Princeton University Press; 2013

[3] Narayanan A, Bonneau J, Felten E, Miller A, Goldfeder S. Bitcoin and Cryptocurrency Technologies: A Comprehensive Introduction. Princeton: Princeton University Press; 2016

[4] Böhme R, Christin N, Edelman B, Bitcoin MT. Economics, technology, and governance. Journal of Economic Perspectives. 2015;**29**(2):213–238. DOI: 10.1257/jep.29.2.213

[5] Jevons WS. Money and the Mechanism of Exchange. New York: D. Appleton and Co; 1876

[6] CoinMarketCap. Bitcoin Historical Price Data. 2024. Available from: https://coinmarketcap.com/currencies/bitcoin/historical-data/ [Accessed: 2026-March-20]

[7] Friedman M. The Quantity Theory of Money—A Restatement. In: Friedman M, editor. Studies in the Quantity Theory of Money. Chicago: University of Chicago Press; 1956. p. 3–21

[8] Mises LV. The Theory of Money and Credit. trans. Batson HE. Indianapolis: Liberty Fund; 1981

[9] Wray LR. Modern Money Theory: A Primer on Macroeconomics for Sovereign monetary/L. 2nd ed. Basingstoke, Hampshire, UK: Randall Wray, University of Missouri-Kansas City, US; 2024

[10] Smith A. An Inquiry into the Nature and Causes of the Wealth of Nations. London: W. Strahan and T. Cadell; 1776

[11] Hayek FA. Denationalisation of Money: The Argument Refined. 3rd ed. London: Institute of Economic Affairs; 1990

[12] Porter ME. How competitive forces shape strategy. Harvard Business Review. 1979;**57**(2):137–145

[13] Porter ME. Competitive Strategy: Techniques for Analyzing Industries and Competitors. New York: Free Press; 1980

[14] Porter ME. Competitive Advantage: Creating and Sustaining Superior Performance. New York: Free Press; 1985

[15] Gorton GB, Zhang JY. Taming wildcat stablecoins. University of Chicago Law Review. 2023;**90**(3): 909–971

[16] Catalini C, Gans JS. Some simple economics of the blockchain. Communications of the ACM. 2020; **63**(7):80–90. DOI: 10.1145/3359552

[17] Chainalysis. The 2022 Crypto Crime Report. New York: Chainalysis Inc.; 2022

[18] Keynes JM. The General Theory of Employment, Interest and Money.

London, United Kingdom: Macmillan Cambridge University Press, for Royal Economic Society; 1936

[19] Baur DG, Hong K, Lee AD. Bitcoin: Medium of exchange or speculative asset? Journal of International Financial Markets, Institutions and Money. 2018;**54**:177–189. DOI: 10.1016/j.intfin.2017.12.004

[20] Corbet S, Hou Y, Hu Y, Larkin C, Lucey B, Oxley L. Cryptocurrency liquidity and volatility interrelationships during the COVID-19 pandemic. Finance Research Letters. 2022;**45**:102137. DOI: 10.1016/j.frl.2021.102137

[21] Cong LW, Li Y, Wang N. Tokenomics: Dynamic adoption and valuation. The Review of Financial Studies. 2021;**34**(3):1105–1155. DOI: 10.1093/rfs/hhaa089

[22] Investing.com. Historical Market Data for Bitcoin, Gold Futures, and S&P 500 Index. https://www.investing.com/ [Accessed: 2026-March-15]

[23] Kahneman D, Tversky A. Prospect theory: An analysis of decision under risk. Econometrica. 1979;**47**(2):263–291. DOI: 10.2307/1914185

[24] Shiller RJ. Narrative Economics: How Stories Go Viral and Drive Major Economic Events. Princeton: Princeton University Press; 2019

[25] Almisshal B, Bulut HI. The dynamics of cryptocurrency market from behavioral finance perspective. Journal of Behavioral and Experimental Finance. 2026;**49**:101126. DOI: 10.1016/j.jbef.2025.101126

[26] Blinder AS. Central-bank credibility: Why do we care? How do we build it? American Economic Review. 2000;**90**(5):1421–1431. DOI: 10.1257/aer.90.5.1421

[27] Bank for International Settlements. Central Bank Digital Currencies: Foundational Principles and Core Features. BIS Report. 2020;1

[28] Auer R, Cornelli G, Frost J Rise of the central bank digital currencies: Drivers, approaches and technologies. BIS Working Papers. 2020;880

[29] Brunnermeier MK, Niepelt D. On the equivalence of private and public money. Journal of Monetary Economics. 2019;**106**:27–41. DOI: 10.1016/j.jmoneco.2019.07.004

[30] Kiyotaki N, Wright R. On money as a medium of exchange. Journal of Political Economy. 1989;**97**(4):927–954. DOI: 10.1086/261634

[31] Bolt W, Van Oordt MRC. On the value of virtual currencies. Journal of Money, Credit and Banking. 2020;**52**(4):835–862. DOI: 10.1111/jmcb.12619

Chapter 4

Risk Management Lessons from Interest Rates

Dieter Lichtenstein

Abstract

When looking at the breakdown between the front-end and the back-end of interest rate markets within the last 30 years, there could be a myriad of catalysts and hindrances that provide a clearer picture of the difference between periods of prosperity versus calamity. While the valuation of the interest rate environment uses data to correctly ascertain the measure, there are also a number of similarities that provide the rationale for why these markets have behaved in this manner. The perspective of risk and return for two varying yield curve durations can potentially be deemed irrelevant, but there is also a strong framework in place to believe that there may be reason to believe in a correlation between the two. Through the work of this paper, the idea will be to confirm the validity and basis of two different theta classes, specifically in this paper, the difference between interest rates, and from there, to determine any level of reciprocity. The approach to measuring any level of variance between the two will be determined by looking through both lenses via a qualitative approach, including external macro conditions, as well as a quantitative approach, including an analysis of annual returns among both classes. Through the combination of these parameters, a further technical approach will be incorporated to gauge potential risk management measures. With the addition of widely practiced risk management as well, the paper will attempt to conclude any relationship between interest rates through the varying lens of the investor.

Keywords: interest rate environment, yield curve, risk management technique, interest rates, term structure

"The expectation of gradual policy normalization should reduce the likelihood of outsized movements in interest rates."

Chairman Jerome Powell (2017)

"One way to think about equity prices is what's the premium you're getting paid to own equities rather than risk-free debt. That's also at fairly low levels, but not extremely low levels. Valuations are high, but not at extremes."

Chairman Jerome Powell (2020)

1. Introduction

When an investor is attempting to find asset and product classes that can best protect the value of their investment, in many situations, one specific class will not embody all the risk that an investor may desire to take across a portfolio. The main goal for all investors is to generate alpha; the dynamics of doing so, however, specifically cater to their investment appetite regarding product and time horizon. Looking through the lens of the traditional investor, there seem to be a few broader markets that can properly capture the overall greater view of the macro environment, and one significant facet includes the fixed-income tranches. While the equity market may receive the most promotional attention from the everyday retail investor, the bond market may arguably be more important, as the total capitalization far supersedes the total asset size within the equity space. There could be a plethora of reasons for this rationale, but bonds may also offer different levels of upside to the investor; they simply do not command the same access to capital as their counterpart in the equity market, however. At year-end 2021, the total size of the US equity market was measured to be roughly $43 trillion,[1] while the total size of the US bond market was measured to be roughly $45 trillion,[2] showing that even though the difference may not be substantial, it is still noticeable to the investor.

For these reasons, a more macro view is more applicable as a comparison basis between classes, and this is where the inclusion of the grander interest rate environment comes into play. In the US economy, the Federal Reserve acts as the largest overseer of the overall interest rate environment, and with this power comes great responsibility. The Fed has made it clear that its foremost concern is yield curve control, which includes a variety of factors such as price stability – a measure that can be easily captured through the movement of interest rates. The overall macro environment can be properly captured by movements in interest rates, momentum that is also generally dictated by the larger central bank of the respective economy. While central banking activity will always be criticized to some degree, to the opposite extent, the behavior will always be respected and priced into the greater valuation of the overall market. This is where factoring in the interest rate market can help in understanding larger movements of the overall environment and can guide the investor toward identifying the best practices for protecting investment capital.

This paper is structured as follows. Section 1 first presents the breakdown of differences between front-end and back-end interest rates and examines the general behavior of the market within the mentioned time frame for these rates. Section 2 analyzes more specific attributes of the interest rates market and compares these through both a quantitative and qualitative approach. Section 3 introduces a more technical categorization of the different yield intervals, as well as an analysis of the most effective risk management techniques. Section 4 provides concluding comments, along with additional ideal practices for the risk-averse investor. Through the information and statistics presented in this paper, it is projected that an

[1] Data compiled from year-end reporting from Securities Industry and Financial Markets Association (SIFMA).

[2] Data compiled from year-end reporting from Securities Industry and Financial Markets Association (SIFMA).

investor will gain a broad understanding of the general dynamics of fixed-income markets and implement the most ideal risk management practices for all future endeavors.

2. Analysis of the yield curve

When investors are looking for the best places to invest their capital (if interest rates and other associated derivatives are their preferred asset class), the idea is generally to find two different durations to deploy capital toward: the front-end of the yield curve versus the back-end of the yield curve. The "short" end, or front-end, of the yield curve tends to refer to short-term securities, usually securities that mature within one year or less. The "long" end, or the back-end, of the yield curve generally refers to longer-duration bonds with maturity dates of 10 years or longer. A third, and arguably most important, component of the yield curve is the "belly" of the curve, which refers to the middle of the curve. The belly can be further composed of the "short end" of the belly, which includes the two-year and three-year marks of the curve, versus the "long end" of the belly, which usually refers to the five-year curve or greater within the 10-year mark.

The takeaway from this section will affirm that there are four substantial yield curve points that can be used to widely gauge investor sentiment. The 10-year Treasury Constant Maturity (10y from here on out) minus the 2-year Constant Maturity (2y from here on out), which takes the difference of the 10y yield subtracted from the 2y yield (referenced as the 2s10s from here on out), reflects a consistent basis from a pricing perspective on what investors may think is an accurate valuation of the frontend/belly of the yield curve. The second yield-curve pairing, the 30-year Treasury Constant Maturity (30y from here on out) minus the 5-year Treasury Constant Maturity (5y from here on out), takes the difference of the 30y yield subtracted from the 5y yield (referenced as the 5s30s from here on out) and can mirror investor sentiment on the belly/back-end of the curve for the overall Treasury market environment.

These two yield-curve pairings tend to be of extreme focus for all investors and traders in the Treasury and interest rates market because so much of the greater economic activity can be encapsulated by the behavior of the moving yields across these curves [1]. It is plausible to consider all 30-year data points that will be further examined in this paper, but for this section, the front-end of the curve, and specifically the points within the 2y and 10y yields, will be considered for further analysis, in conjunction with the 5y and 30y yields for a back-end of the curve analysis.

With a more fundamental understanding now exhibited, it is possible to do a deeper dive into the specific analysis between the actual front-end of the yield curve versus the back-end, which will serve as the core of this paper. One of the most important foundational concepts for this is the term structure model, which essentially describes the trajectory of all interest rates [2]. Before investigating the specific analysis of both ends of the yield curve, we must also confirm the general dynamics of the overall term structure of interest rates. When looking at the term structure of the overall bond market, two parameters must be considered and quantified: the yield-to-maturity, which should be expressed in percentage points, and the time to maturity, which should be expressed in years. The term structure is

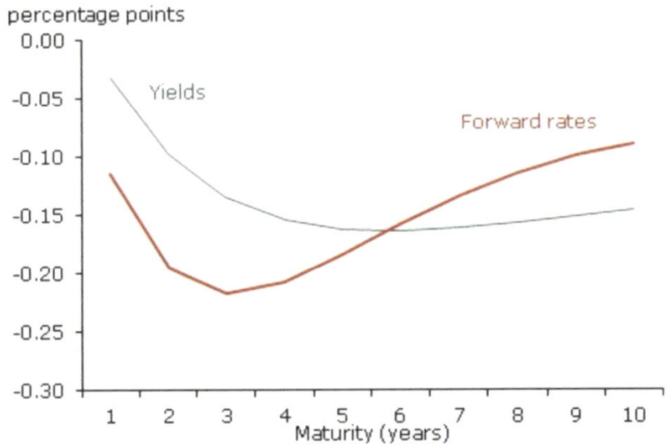

Figure 1.
Term structure of interest rates, per Federal Reserve Bank of San Francisco [4].

drawn for each specified point in time, with each point including the yield-to-maturity as well as the term to maturity [3].

By looking at the above **Figure 1**[3] one theme becomes immediately clear to the investor – the downward-sloping nature of the term structure confirms the idea that short-term yields are higher than long-term yields. For the entire yield curve, we will examine a more detailed analysis of these curve points later in the paper, but it is important to establish the underlying parameters of said points. Even though the upward-sloping yield curve may be more common in general investing environments than the downward-sloping yield curve, the downward-sloping yield curve is consistent with the current world economic landscape: interest rates have been declining while the price of long-term bonds has been rising.

There is also another pair of factors that must be considered when looking at the term structure of Treasury bonds: investment quality and tax exposure [5]. Investment quality may most accurately represent the given coupon on a bond, and with an ascending coupon rate per bond, it can also entail many other different conditions that must be accounted for with respect to the increasing rate compared to other similar securities. Tax exposure largely depends on domicile, and while the United States can strongly be considered an established economy that can pay down its obligations, the same, unfortunately, cannot be said for some of its other established peers. This is a key characteristic that all investors must account for when making the decision on the basis of Treasury investment [6].

A final overview of the term structure must be analyzed before moving to the analysis of the 2s10s curve and the 5s30s curve. Predominantly speaking, there are three external factors that can contribute to the shape of any given term structure: expectations, premium, and inefficiency. Market expectations largely refer to the future direction of interest rates, and this idea is captured in the market expectations theory; the market expectations theory portrays the idea that the term structure is influenced largely by expectations, and the yield-to-maturity of a 5-year bond is calculated as the average yield of 1-year bonds over a 5-year period [7]. The presence of liquidity premia in the market can also influence bond returns, and this is encapsulated

[3] The majority of interest rate environment data will be derived from Federal Reserve Economic Data and its affiliated entities unless specified otherwise.

in the liquidity preference theory: the liquidity preference theory interprets the premium derived from risk parameters and further conveys the idea that the shape of the term structure is affected by a variety of factors, some of which include market expectations for short-term rates, as well as any presence of premia on either short- or long-term bonds [8]. Potential inefficiency in the market is the third characteristic covered, and the market segmentation theory attempts to confirm these segments. The market segmentation theory remains consistent with the idea of inefficiency with respect to the pricing of bonds and maintains that each maturity tenor of the bond market should be considered segmented into its own bucket [7].

By conducting a deeper analysis of various topics within the broader interest rate environment, such as the different segments of the yield curve and risk management models focused on interest rates and derivatives, we can begin to investigate a more specific study of the movement of the 2s10s curve and the 5s30s curve. Through this exploration, we can break down more applicable risk management techniques, such as stress testing and modeling limit usage, to further identify the risk and return associated with this section of the yield curve and start to uncover the underlying causes of its behavior over the past 30 years.

3. Breakdown of interest rates yields

When comparing the breakdown of interest rates, it can be important to look at the overall broader view through two different perspectives: quantitative and qualitative. While many investors would argue that simply looking at a chart for the respective securities is sufficient to categorize an investment as worthy of deploying capital toward, it is also necessary to look at the larger macroeconomic environment and see what nonsystematic factors could be at play within the investment horizon. By looking at the largest picture of data possible, combined between both factors, the investor can properly attribute which risk management technique would prove most feasible.

The first subsection of this section will thoroughly analyze the statistical tracking of the greater interest rates market over the past 30 years, specifically focusing on the 2s10s curve.

The first chart to be examined will be the yield of the 2-year Treasury rate (**Figure 2**). While there are more crucial immediate short-term rates that are focused on exclusively, such as the overnight rate, the 3-month Treasury rate, and perhaps the 1-year Treasury rate, the 2-year could perhaps (from a front-end perspective) be considered the most important yield metric, due to the fact that the 2y is such a common leg for a pairs trade in interest rates trading. While the institutional flow desk certainly has the utmost focus on 3-month and 1-year rates, the 2-year rate is significantly scrutinized due to its apparent level of sensitivity to the other yield points.[4]

The next chart of interest will investigate the yield of the 10-year Treasury rate (**Figure 3**). The 10y could widely be considered the most important interest rate yield for all investors, whether they focus on equities, fixed-income, or a different asset class. Regardless of focus, this is a yield point of paramount importance.

[4] At of the time of this writing (early November 2022), the yield curve has been trading under a dramatic period of duress, with the 2y hitting a 15-year high mark.

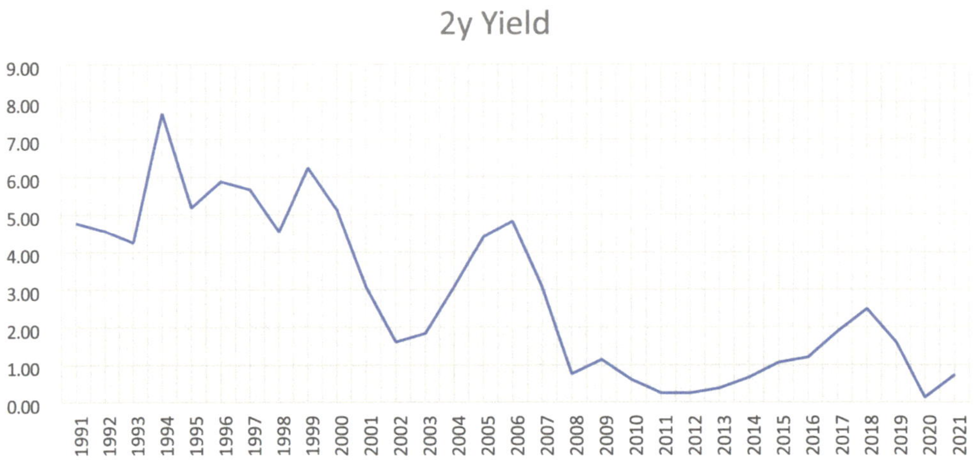

Figure 2.
Yield (in basis points) for the 2-year Treasury [4].

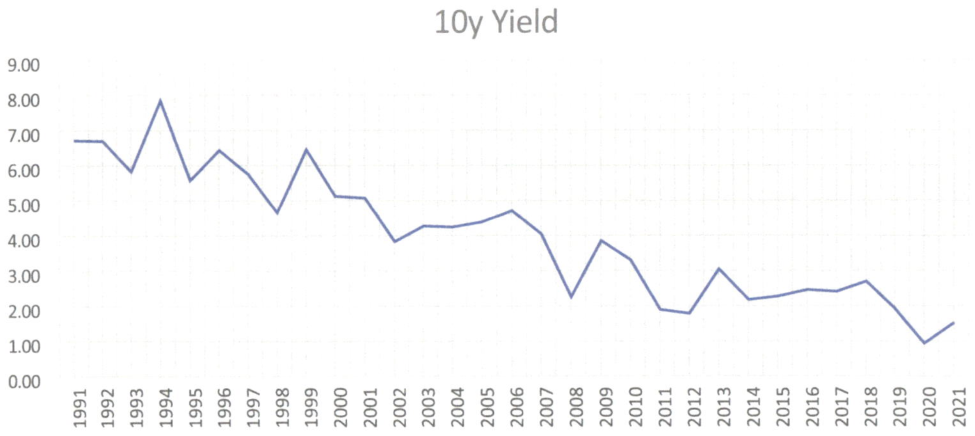

Figure 3.
Yield (in basis points) for the 10-year Treasury [4].

Considered to be the belly of the yield curve, the 10y may potentially have the best bearing on the overall grasp of the interest rate environment.

When initially examining the graph of the 10y, many similar themes may appear obvious to the investor. For the past 30 years, from a yield perspective, the greater interest rate environment has seen periods of decline; while this may initially appear as a weakness, in the grand scheme of things, this would imply that the strength of the bond market has continued, a factor which may grant more durability to the vitality of the overall fixed-income market. Even though many of the parameters that are scrutinized in the overall fixed-income atmosphere are not as heavily critiqued as parameters within the interest rate environment, most of these factors end up being completely priced into the overall picture of the yield curve, and whether the direction of said yield curve ultimately results in an upward or downward-facing slope [9].

Annual year	2y (ending) rate	10y (ending) rate
1991	4.77%	6.71%
1992	4.56%	6.70%
1993	4.25%	5.83%
1994	7.69%	7.84%
1995	5.18%	5.58%
1996	5.88%	6.43%
1997	5.66%	5.75%
1998	4.54%	4.65%
1999	6.24%	6.45%
2000	5.11%	5.12%
2001	3.07%	5.07%
2002	1.61%	3.83%
2003	1.84%	4.27%
2004	3.08%	4.24%
2005	4.41%	4.39%
2006	4.82%	4.71%
2007	3.05%	4.04%
2008	0.76%	2.25%
2009	1.14%	3.85%
2010	0.61%	3.30%
2011	0.25%	1.89%
2012	0.25%	1.78%
2013	0.38%	3.04%
2014	0.67%	2.17%
2015	1.06%	2.27%
2016	1.20%	2.45%
2017	1.89%	2.40%
2018	2.48%	2.69%
2019	1.58%	1.92%
2020	0.13%	0.93%
2021	0.73%	1.52%

Table 1.
Chart detailing specific yields for the 2-year Treasury and the 10-year Treasury [4].

Looking at both charts for the 2y and the 10y, there are certainly some years in which the yield points move in definitive tandem. While we will shortly investigate themes and strategies for why this may have occurred, it is important to identify if any larger external circumstances could be at play because of this overall behavior.

Through the yields specified in **Table 1**, it may be easier to decipher the market events that led to this point. Notable years that initially stick out to the reader may include 1994, 1999, 2002, 2008, and 2020. Broadly speaking, there were a multitude of economic events going on in the world, but these years may point to even larger circumstances in the broader interest rate environment.

To begin, in 1994, a massive crisis in the bond market, known as the "Bond Massacre," produced a significant decline in bond market prices across the entire fixed-income atmosphere. While in the year leading up to this, in 1993, bonds were enjoying a bull run that resulted in strong returns for several investors across the space, the back-end of the curve (specifically the 30-year) was adjusted to combat this.

Treasury rates had the potential to see further inclination; thus, one of the first battles from the Federal Reserve to combat inflation would ensue [10]. When the effect of the crash was seen, Chairman Alan Greenspan made the decision to increase the Federal funds target by 25 basis points, from 3% to 3.25%. This would serve as the first gesture made by the Federal Reserve to attempt to restrain the money supply for nearly five years, since 1985 [3]. This motion set into place a period where dramatic short-term increases would be seen on front-end yields, with the 2y increase increasing by more than 300 basis points on a year-over-year basis, and rates that would not decline to the prior 1993 level for quite some time – until nearly a decade later [4].

The next period of focus, in 1999, could also be construed due to several factors involved in the overall market. While the Internet sector of stock booms will be discussed later, of importance for this section is explaining the setup of the booming decade of the 1990s. While previously looked upon in 1994, the large disparity among the 2y yields in 1999–2001[5] can widely be attributed to the economic success of the 1990s [11]. Specifically for the bond market, outside of the hiccup in the early 1990s, the bull market was in full swoon, with levels of regulation still not nearly in place to the level which would eventually be reached in the modern era. Volatility in the bond market contributed to further erratic movement within the front-end of the yield curve during this time period.

The year beginning in 2002 can be recognized as the beginning of the aftermath of the tumultuous time leading up to and from 1998 onwards. When looking at overall investment firm activity during this time period, something significantly important to raise is the downfall of a prominent hedge fund, Long-Term Capital Management.[6] While the greater collapse of the firm has been detailed in full previously, one important distinction to add is the effect the firm had on the Thai Baht and Russian Ruble, which would indirectly affect all currency and macro markets from then on into the next few years. To briefly summarize, in 1997, a sort of Asian Financial Crisis endured, which has been largely attributed to the lack of foreign currency to support its own currency peg to the US Dollar, and in 1998, the Russian Central Bank had to default on its own debt and thus devalue the Ruble due to the sovereign's inability to pay down its debt [10]. Both of these larger currency collapses can be directly attributed to the failure of Long Term Capital Management (LTCM), as well as the short-term downfall of Treasury yields.

[5] Outside of periods of extreme volatility, interest rate yields do not regularly see consistent 100 basis point moves in either direction on a year-over-year basis.

[6] A wonderful paper titled *Risk Management Lessons from Long-Term Capital Management* by Phillippe Jorion served as an indirect influence of this paper and should be sufficiently studied for all future investors in the risk management or trading space.

When looking at 2008, this may also appear to be a year in which several negative key economic events were unfolding around the world. The most prominent of these events was the Great Recession, a period during which an inadequate level of due diligence by institutional investors failed to properly identify the incoming subprime mortgage crisis. This crisis had a dramatic effect on yields from here, with the 2y seeing more than a 200 basis point decline, and the 10y, in turn, experiencing a similar level of decline, even though this same 200 basis point threshold was thankfully not crossed [12]. This period saw the most extreme decline in yield curve behavior, and the levels seen decimated here would not be reached again for a substantial period of time.

The final age that bears analysis is the year 2020. While those alive during this period certainly know the trials and tribulations that society as a whole endured, what many people may not be aware of is the dramatic volatility seen in the overall interest rate environment. Yields cratered to more than 100 basis point losses on both the 2y and the 10y, and the 2y even nearly saw the yield flirt with either 0% or negative rates for a brief moment in time [12]. While the low on the 2y specifically never crossed below 0%, 10 basis points (the approximate lowest point reached this year) is never a level of yield that investors would deem adequate for an investor in the space. While the current interest rate environment has largely recovered from this precipitous drop, there have been levels of volatility not seen in a number of years.[7] There are still factors that need to be addressed in order to see the full strength of the greater US economy.

While looking at the above chart that compares the yield of the 2y versus the yield of the 10y (**Figure 4**), there may be a number of years that stand out. To begin, the 2y yield largely remains below the 10y yield, with the exception of extreme

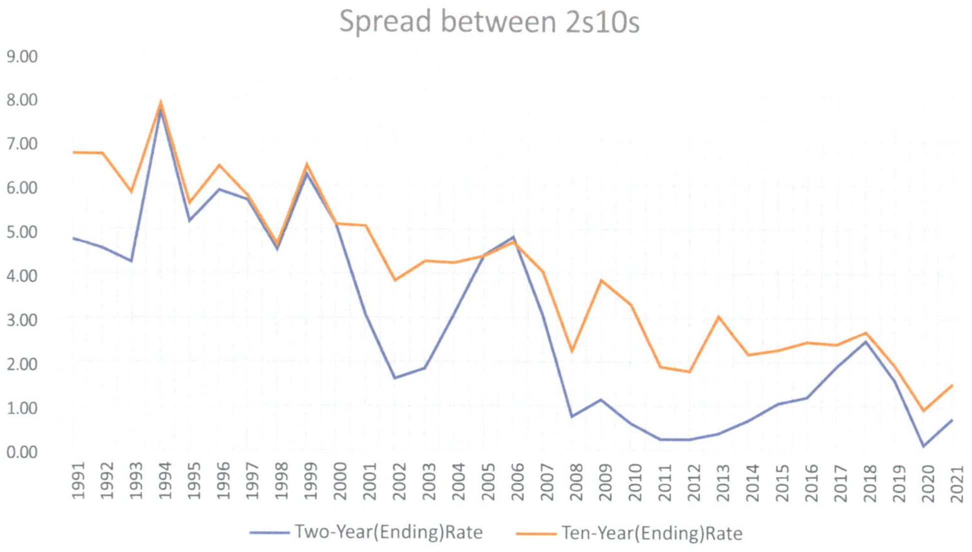

Figure 4.
Spread level among 2y and 10y curve points [4].

[7] As of the time of this writing (early November 2022), the 2y has currently fixed to 5.026% and the 10y has currently fixed to 4.161%.

situations. Many of these plot points serve as immediate indicators before either a recessionary event or even greater economic calamity may occur.[8] The near level of inversion in 1994, 1999, and 2018 affirmed dire calamities to be seen in the future by the broader interest rate environment. The inversion of 2006 proved to be the ultimate indicator of some of the greatest levels of weakness that markets have seen in recent history, and in future years, there could be a reasonable expectation to see a similar inversion come to fruition in the market. Even though general best practices to prevent these measures are applied by all Central Banks, they may not be able to handle the situation until it has spiraled out of control. Unfortunately for the common investor, it may be too late to adequately practice risk management techniques once the situation has been alleviated.

The next subsection of this section will analyze the behavior of the greater interest rates market over the past 30 years, specifically focusing on the 5s30s curve.

The next chart to be inspected will be the yield of the 5-year Treasury rate (**Figure 5**). Considered one of the most prominent points of the belly of the curve, the 5y and 10y yields are frequently considered together as pair points, even though the 5s10s curve itself is not necessarily as prominent as either the 2s10s curve or the 5s30s curve [3]. While the 5y does not serve as the same level of benchmark for other borrowing rates as the 10y or other curve points, the 5y itself still sits within arguably the most important section of the yield curve.

Serving as the second important leg of the 5s30s curve is the 30y yield point. While maintaining the levels of strength and weakness from the back-end of the curve may not always be the strongest point of focus for the Federal Reserve and other central banks, it is still important to properly follow the patterns that this chart could reveal to the investor. While inflationary concerns[9] tend to be the focus overall with respect to protecting the term structure of interest rates, the back-end of the

Figure 5.
Yield (in basis points) for the 5-year Treasury [4].

[8] As of the time of this writing, the current 2s10s is seeing an extreme level of inversion, indicating nearly a full 100 basis point inversion.

[9] During the time of this writing (November 2022), the Fed has made it clear that their foremost concern is easing the widespread effects of inflation throughout the country. In their belief, the most direct way of maintaining this has (so far) been consistently increasing the Fed Funds rate.

Figure 6.
Yield (in basis points) for the 30-year Treasury [4].

curve may not have the strongest implications for these immediate measures [9]. However, this does not defeat the purpose of maintaining the 30y levels.

The next chart of interest will investigate the yield of the 30-year Treasury rate (**Figure 6**). The 30y may be the least researched curve of all four curve points in this paper but still demonstrates a strong correlation to broader yield curve movements as well. There are a variety of ways in which an investor could measure duration, but analysis of the 30y could prove to be the most prominent, depending on the focus of trading.

As seen within the curve points for the 30y, it is clear that this point follows many similarities to its predecessors, although some of the years within the 30y may not have experienced as severe a movement in volatility as the 5y specifically, but also within the 2y and 10y. One important distinction here could be that many fixed-income investors feel a semblance of a "safe haven" from a yield that sits at the farthest back-end of the yield curve, and because of this, general volatility may not be as severe for the 30y compared to prior points [5].

When looking at the initial charting of the 5y and 30y yields, it is clear that these points have a nearly identical correlation to their counterparts among the 2y and 10y yields. While it is obvious that all points based on the same curve should move jointly relative to one another, the specific level of movement may not always prove to be the same.

While looking at the specific data points above for both the 5y and 30y (**Table 2**), it seems clear that the underlying fundamental movement among interest rates has remained constant over the past 30 years. When conducting the initial analysis for the 2y and 10y, some significant years stood out as potential outliers: 1994, 1999, 2002, 2008, and 2020. Looking at the chart above, these same years appear to hold true with respect to time periods of significant economic stress.

In 1994, the "Bond Massacre" previously described confirmed the decline across all resulting Treasury yields over the past 30 years. While some of the moves across the prior curves were more extreme than the 5s30s curve, there are still clear signs of extreme volatility within these years. Movements of greater than 200 basis points are clearly not standard trading, and the 5s30s followed suit from the 2s10s in this move during the early years of the 1990s [10].

Annual year	5y (ending) rate	10y (ending) rate
1991	5.93%	7.41%
1992	6.04%	7.40%
1993	5.21%	6.35%
1994	7.83%	7.89%
1995	5.38%	5.96%
1996	6.21%	6.65%
1997	5.71%	5.93%
1998	4.56%	5.09%
1999	6.36%	6.48%
2000	4.99%	5.46%
2001	4.38%	5.48%
2002	2.78%	5.80%
2003	3.25%	4.81%
2004	3.63%	5.07%
2005	4.35%	4.82%
2006	4.70%	4.81%
2007	3.45%	4.45%
2008	1.55%	2.69%
2009	2.69%	4.63%
2010	2.01%	4.34%
2011	0.83%	2.89%
2012	0.72%	2.95%
2013	1.75%	3.96%
2014	1.65%	2.75%
2015	1.76%	3.01%
2016	1.93%	3.06%
2017	2.20%	2.74%
2018	2.51%	3.02%
2019	1.69%	2.39%
2020	0.36%	1.65%
2021	1.26%	1.93%

Table 2.
Chart detailing specific yields for the 5-year Treasury and the 30-year Treasury [4].

Looking upon the next noticeable year of 1999, a similar instance can be seen as before. After the return to normal around 1995 from the previous surge in 1994, which includes a single-digit spread among the 5s30s curve, it is reasonable to believe that the same economic conditions that affected the 2s10s curve also affected the 5s30s curve. While 1999 saw a mere 12 basis point spread among the 5s30s, simply waiting two more years would see this curve point return to a period of normalcy previously seen in the chart [10].

Following into 2002, the similar themes of currency implosion can be seen as beginning to alter movement in the resulting years. Observing the spread among the 5s30s reveals one of the most severe spreads of the period, indicating that perhaps the back-end of the curve experienced more substantial movement than the front-end of the curve during this time [10].

For the year 2008, this will truly serve as one of the worst financial performances of all asset classes, with the exception of leveraged loans providing the only semblance of positive performance throughout the entire financial ecosystem. While the spread here narrowed to one of the tighter levels seen in recent years, this would not prove to be beneficial for the overall economy during this time.

The final year in question, 2020, also proved to show similar results across the yield curve as a whole. While the spread began to experience a retracement back to more standard levels, the true effects of this overall interest rate environment would not be more widely observed until the near future. The next year alone saw nearly a halving of the prior year's spread[10] and the chart would concede to that point not potentially changing.

While looking at the above chart on the 5s30s comparison (**Figure 7**), many similar years of peril from the 2s10s confirm validity among the same years. While inversion among these points does not appear as common as points of inversion for the 2s10s, there are similar periods that come close to the same level [6]. 1994 saw a period of the lone single-digit spread for the 5s30s, which was also a significant year for the 2s10s spread. Other poorly performing years would not reach this same level of near inversion, as this scenario would not occur in general to see a complete inversion across the curve in the near future years. While this may confirm the fact that duration holds up stronger in periods of volatility, generally speaking, periods of duress remain constant across all curve points [3].

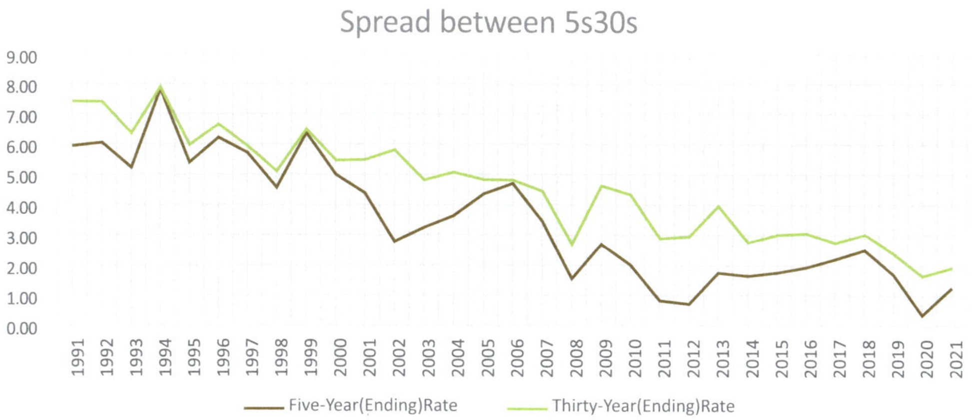

Figure 7.
Spread levels among 5y and 30y curve points [4].

[10] While at the time of this writing, the 5s30s curve has not inverted similar to its counterpart in the 2s10s curve, the overall fixed-income market has seen sustained weakness throughout year-end 2022.

By conducting a more comprehensive analysis of various topics within specifically defined risk management practices, we can delve into a more detailed breakdown of the interest rate environment and how such investments need to be adequately addressed from a risk management perspective. Through the exploration of this analysis, we can identify more applicable risk management techniques to better assess the risk and return in relation to the yield curve and begin to uncover the underlying causes of behavior observed over the past 30 years.

4. Comparison among risk management factors

Within the breakdown of the curve, most risk management strategies can be characterized under two umbrellas: equilibrium models and arbitrage models. Equilibrium models attempt to define economic variables and derive the true valuation for the proper rate, which can more clearly define the different price points for bonds, options, as well as other products within the interest rate space [1]. Furthermore, there are several submodels characterized within equilibrium models, which include the Rendelman and Bartter Model: a model that assumes the short-term interest rate behaves like a stock price, although this may be an inaccurate comparison because of the general mean reversion of interest rates over a longrun average level across a broad duration; the Vasicek Model, a more nuanced version of the Rendelman and Bartter Model that consolidates mean reversion within the model, accurately portraying the picture that high interest rates have a negative trend and low interest rates have a positive trend; and the Cox, Ingersoll, and Ross Model: a model that essentially follows similar ideals of mean reversion as the Rendelman and Bartter Model but also introduces the concept of the standard deviation, accurately capturing any movement across short-term interest rates [1].

Additionally, there is another group of No-Arbitrage models that may more accurately portray the current environment regarding the term structure of interest rates [1]. These include the Ho-Lee Model: the first no-arbitrage model of its kind that examines the short-rate standard deviation versus the market price of risk in the short rate; the Hull–White Model: a model that serves as a de facto extension of the Vasicek Model with an added component of a time-dependent reversion level; the Black–Derman-Toy Model: a more technical, statistically-based model that includes a factor ensuring the interest rate never becomes negative; and the Black–Karasinski Model: a model that serves as an extension of the Black–Derman–Toy Model where the rate of reversion is characterized as a separate peripheral of the formula.[11]

After researching the broader economic outlook within the interest rate environment, the next topic that must be addressed is what should be the most important risk management technique in order to properly assess the valuation, as well as potential return metrics and risk parameters, for the market. While there is a myriad of risk management techniques that risk managers use on a daily basis, the most crucial risk management techniques to be analyzed include value at risk (VaR), stress tests, Profit and Loss (PnL) sensitivity, and limit usage.

Value at risk may be the most commonly referred to risk management technique, and this measure refers to the "loss corresponding to a very low percentile of the entire return distribution . . . or another name for the quantile of a distribution." [2]

[11] A terrific breakdown of Interest Rate Derivatives is characterized in *Options, Futures, and Other Derivatives*, by John C. Hull. The general breakdown has been excerpted from his exceptional work here.

In other words, VaR attempts to quantify the largest possible extent of financial losses that could occur within a portfolio over a specific period of time. Through the use of specific definitions within probability, as well as confidence intervals, VaR can accurately measure any duration necessary, whether it be across the 2s10s curve or the 5s30s curve.

Stress testing is another risk management technique that attempts to quantify best efforts at calculating potential losses. The main concept within stress testing is to sufficiently assess "whether banks are capitalized to absorb losses during stressful conditions while meeting obligations to creditors and counterparties and continuing to be able to lend to ... businesses" [7]. PnL sensitivity, with respect to risk management, largely refers to underlying movements within the options Greeks, and, for the purpose of this paper, will not be examined further.[12] From the perspective of the interest rate environment, one of the most important concepts within stress testing is ensuring that all scenarios adequately capture the interest rate risk in the banking book.

A final risk management technique, limit usage, gauges the potential thresholds under certain umbrellas, such as credit risk, market risk, or liquidity risk, and attempts to define specific buckets within which trading can be undertaken before breaching a certain upper or lower limit [3]. While there are a variety of factors that may affect each specific facet within limit usage differently, the idea remains that breaching any of these parameters can adversely affect an investor's portfolio. When discussing the term structure of interest rates, each of these three buckets of risk can drastically alter the valuation of a portfolio.

When researching the potential outlook of the yield curve and the greater interest rate environment, arguably the most applicable risk management technique could be considered stress testing. With the passing of the Financial Crisis, the Federal Reserve understood the need to increase efforts in balance sheet control, as well as yield curve control. While Dodd–Frank was a massive new law introduced into daily sales and trading, another strategy that was implemented was the Comprehensive Capital Analysis and Review (CCAR) [4]. While the stress test may be a more forward-looking figure, the CCAR is more so considered a combination of qualitative and quantitative assessments looking back on historical data. The qualitative component includes measures such as whether institutions were adequately prepared for any adverse situation unique to their circumstances, while the quantitative component examines the capital commitments of institutions and the degree to which an institution would be able to continue daily operations under dynamic periods of duress.

One important concept to evaluate is researching prior periods of extreme volatility and investigating the spreads on the 2s10s and 5s30s curves. For 1994, the spread was 15 basis points for the 2s30s and 6 basis points for the 5s30s; for 1999, the spread was 21 basis points for the 2s30s and 12 basis points for the 5s30s; for 2002, the spread was 222 basis points for the 2s10s and 302 basis points for the 5s30s; for 2008, the spread was 149 basis points for the 2s10s and 114 basis points for the 5s30s; and for 2020, the spread was 80 basis points for the 2s10s and 129 basis points for the 5s30s [4]. Looking at these numbers, some immediate inferences can be made: spreads have increased dramatically as time has continued, an assessment that can likely be attributed to growing balance sheet concerns for the

[12] Adding the elements of delta, gamma, kappa, and theta movements, while integral for daily trading for an Options trading desk, is too large to implement within the topic of this paper.

USA, liquidity concerns over several products and asset classes, as well as overall market risk with dwindling confidence in overall central banking activity.

By incorporating the risk management technique of stress testing, if a risk manager were properly measuring and attaining risk through their portfolio, then there are several assumptions that could be made from the prior periods rather than the aforementioned significant years mentioned before.

For example, in 1993, the spread between the 2s10s was significant (more than 100 basis points) but had still shrunk dramatically from the prior year in 1992 (more than 200 basis points). When looking at the 5s30s, in 1993 the spread was fairly wide (more than 100 basis points) but then reverted back closer to a single-digit standard compared to 1992. While periods of contagion can at times surprise investors, a sufficient risk manager would have likely been able to gauge the pattern of the narrowing spread from 1992 and 1993 and foreseen a disastrous event coming to the interest rate environment in 1994 [4].

Furthermore, in 1999, there were countless underlying issues in all markets. While the equity market was the key offender during this time period, largely thanks to the late 1990s Internet boom, there were also clear contagion factors worldwide that could have been prevented through the use of proper risk management techniques in tangential markets as well. While the crises underpinning the Asian and Russian economies were certainly at the forefront, there were still clear-cut factors, such as looking at the 2s10s and 5s30s spreads, that could indicate potential strength or weakness [4]. Through stress testing, a risk manager could see the number of standard deviations outside of the norm happening within the early 1990s, and it could have been adequately determined that a similar situation was brewing toward the late 1990s.

While the period surrounding 2002 has somewhat different circumstances than the prior periods of 1994 and 1999, there is still reason to believe that the use of stress testing or VaR could have proven to be an efficient risk management technique during this time. While the period of volatility was certainly staggering (2s10s spread of 1 basis point in 2000, followed by 200 basis points in 2001; 5s30s spread of 47 basis points in 2000, followed by 110 basis points in 2001)[13] there are also reasons to believe it could have potentially been forecasted through risk management [4]. When looking at prior periods through the 1992–2002 decade, 7 of these 10 years ended in a double-digit basis point spread, so after the dramatic rise in 2001, this should have served as a catalyst for further potential calamity in the interest rate environment. Including the composition of VaR, a risk manager could have determined that these spreads were not favorable compared to previous historical data.

Moving forward to 2008, a similar practice in yield curve control could have potentially been measured during this time. While the practice of targeting the back end of the yield curve and then either buying or selling the treasuries of that curve can effectively control movements within the yield curve, this practice was not attainable in 2008. It is fair to say that the subprime mortgage crisis was a significant surprise to investors, falling outside an extreme standard deviation. However, through a similar exercise of back testing, looking at prior years could have again indicated a potential downturn for a risk management professional. By looking at a larger-than-100-basis-point spread in 2004 for the 2s10s versus a secondary

[13] It is fair to say that this type of market movement would severely fall outside of 99% of standard deviations within a similar portfolio during this time.

substantial spread of nearly 150 basis points for the 5s30s, followed by back-to-back years of the yield curve inverting, followed by another greater-than-100-basis-point spread, it seems reasonable that 2008 could be pinpointed as a year of potential pain through the use of stress testing as well as VaR measures [4].

Finally, we come to the year 2020. It is logical to conclude that less than 0.1% of the population could have foreseen a pandemic that would rival its biggest predecessor since 1918 unraveling in the world, but that does not mean that risk management techniques could not still have been implemented in place leading up to the event. Questionable decision-making from the Federal Reserve and its affiliates led to similar patterns seen in prior years, but again, there always tends to be an outlier. Spreads for these curves were seen at levels flirting around 100 basis points. However, due to both the Presidential administration's pressure as well as reactionary behavior from the Federal Reserve, the 2s10s spread tightened back into double digits, along with a noticeable tightening among the 5s30s spread, coming to the closest level of inversion of 21 basis points in 2018 [4]. While it is unnecessary and redundant to attempt to revise history due to political differences, the risk manager can, in fact, revise portfolios due to stress testing. Even though the worst levels of the spread would not be seen until the near future,[14] using scenario analyses of the past two decades could have indicated that the interest rate environment had not yet felt the highest level of pain.

5. Conclusion

While there are certainly a number of factors that can be adequately used as a risk management technique, the most conclusive factor for the practice of properly maintaining the most efficient yield curve can be attributed to stress testing. By using past numbers within history as potential factors for future performance, this approach can provide the risk manager with tools to properly protect a portfolio. Through this examination, the risk manager would be able to test several different scenarios falling on several different levels of threshold crossings and limit usages to properly ascertain the valuation of the portfolio.

Even though stress testing could be considered the most effective risk management technique, a variety of other techniques can be effective as well when managing risk across the yield curve. While VaR may be more common across other asset classes, there is still clear usage among interest rates. By specifying key elements across the yield curve, such as a specific potential loss value, a fixed period of time for the determination, and a confidence interval, VaR can also adequately assist risk managers in the proper analysis of their portfolio.

Through the implementation of these risk management techniques, other valuable pricing models, and a general strong understanding of underlying fundamentals within interest rates, any weaknesses in an investor's portfolio can be identified and further prevented from causing any downside. By properly defining risk parameters and buckets, each of the techniques – through stress testing, VaR, limit usage, and PnL sensitivity – can affirmatively identify any potential breaches in the portfolio. Through proper management of arbitrage and pricing models, an investor can further support the protection of their investments and adequately

[14] As of the time of this writing (early November 2022), the 2s10s spread continues to remain inverted and this is not trending in the direction of a reversal anytime soon.

prepare themselves for any downside. Finally, an investor should always be aware of the specific product they are investing in. By effectively comparing and researching these risks, the implication is that the investor can sufficiently protect themselves from any inefficiencies or unforeseen circumstances in the overall market.

Author details

Dieter Lichtenstein
Independent Researcher, New York, USA

*Address all correspondence to: dclichtenstein@gmail.com

References

[1] Hull JC. Options, Futures, and Other Derivatives. Upper Saddle River, New Jersey, Pearson; 2017. p. 706–728

[2] Hull JC. Fundamentals of Futures and Options Markets. Upper Saddle River, New Jersey, Pearson; 2008. p. 433–458

[3] Baisalova A, Loiseau-Aslanidi O, Alpizar L, Luis J, Solis Gonzalez B. Embedding Interest Rate Risk into Stress Testing: Macroeconomic Scenarios in Behavioral Models. Moody's Rating Corporation: 2021. Available from: https://www.moodys.com/web/en/us/insights/banking/embedding-interest-rate-risk-into-stress-testing.html

[4] Board of Governors of the Federal Reserve System (U.S). The Federal Reserve System. Washington, D.C: Board of Governors; 2022

[5] Cecchetti SG, Schoenholtz KL. Money, Banking, and Financial Markets. New York, NY: McGraw-Hill Education; 2014. p. 70–78

[6] Madura J. Financial Markets and Institutions. Fort Lauderdale, FL: Cengage Learning; 2008. p. 421435

[7] Haugen RA. Modern Investment Theory. Upper Saddle River, New Jersey: Prentice Hall International; 1986. p. 367–402

[8] Bodie Z, Kane A, Marcus A. Investments. Vol. **138**. New York, NY: McGraw-Hill Education; 2009. p. 140–145

[9] Thorbecke W. Why deficity news affects interest rates. Journal of Policy Modeling. 1993;**15**(1):1–11

[10] Kolchin K, Podziemska J, Hadley D. Capital Markets Fact Book. 2022

[11] Liu Z, Miao J, Dongling S. Fiscal Stimulus Under Average Inflation Targeting. Federal Reserve Bank of San Francisco Working Paper 2022-22. 2022

[12] Hillebrand S. The Fed and the Secular Decline in Interest Rates. November 21, 2022. Available from: https://ssrn.com/abstract=3550593

Chapter 5

Hong Kong Currency Board and the 2008 Global Financial Crisis

Chee-Heong Quah and Yew Joe Ho

Abstract

In light of the imported boom-bust cycle that frequently beleaguers the small open economy of Hong Kong, it is persuasive to evaluate the health of this dollar-linked currency board following the Great Financial Crisis of 2008. Along this line, this chapter compares the circumstances of Hong Kong in recent times with those leading to the 2002 currency board crisis of Argentina. The time period examined for Hong Kong is 2000–2016, the period including the US subprime episode, while that for Argentina is 1991–2001, the lifetime of its pegged dollar regime. Dimensions explored are adherence to currency board principles, economic performance in aspects pertinent to the fixed exchange rate regime, and conformity to criteria motivated by optimum currency areas theory. In a nutshell, findings do not suggest any path that will lead to an Argentine-type crisis for Hong Kong. Substantive differences are observed in the two economies' adherence to currency board principles. While both engaged in sterilization operations deviating from orthodox currency board rules, Hong Kong's abundant foreign reserves sustained market confidence, as evidenced by the close convergence of money market interest rates with those of the United States. In terms of macroeconomic performance, Hong Kong maintained stable growth, low inflation, and a strong external position, in contrast to Argentina's declining competitiveness and debt-financed current account deficits. Moreover, Hong Kong exhibits greater conformity with optimum currency area criteria, particularly in trade openness and business-cycle synchronization with the United States, reinforcing the resilience of its dollar-linked regime.

Keywords: Argentina, currency board, Hong Kong, dollar, money

1. Introduction

Even after more than a decade, world economies are still beleaguered by the shadow of the 2008–09 global financial crisis that originated in the United States. Hong Kong, which in practice ties its Hong Kong dollar exchange rate to the US dollar, has recently received much attention in the money and banking literature. For instance, even at the cost of a higher price level, Tam [1] finds that a free-floating exchange rate regime may instead bring Hong Kong the benefit of smaller output variation at a higher level of output than that brought about by the present currency board regime. On the other hand, Lo [2] argues that Hong Kong's small open economy is susceptible to international forces, so anchoring its exchange rate to the US dollar, a world currency in trade and finance, remains a practical way of bolstering market confidence and reducing volatilities in the economy.

Indeed, Hong Kong has shown a track record of economic resiliency in times of financial distress, as demonstrated during the 1997–1998 Asian crisis (see, e.g., [3]). Many have attributed this trait to its robust dollar-linked exchange rate regime, which makes the HK dollar impossible for speculators to prey on. In spite of this, as Chen [4] finds, during most of the Asian crisis period, the HK dollar was actually supported by its huge foreign reserves instead of the currency board. At that time of turbulence, billions of dollars would have flowed in and out of Hong Kong via electronic transfers without ever involving its currency board, which was based on notes and coins.

In fact, the rigid exchange regime could have actually made Hong Kong exceptionally vulnerable to foreign shocks, especially those coming from the United States. During periods of boom, credit expansions and asset bubbles in the United States would easily spill over to Hong Kong almost instantaneously [5]. The resulting overheating would then force local authorities to tighten lending and financial regulations, which could distort genuine lending and business activities. As for periods of bust following a shock, tensions in the HK interbank money market would rise virtually concurrently with those in the United States [6].

Skepticisms have also arisen over whether a stable price level has been achieved by subscribing to the US monetary policy. For instance, Devereux [7] discovers that, since the 1983 inception of the currency board through the 1997–98 Asian crisis, Hong Kong had to endure significantly higher price inflation than that in the United States. Also, the lack of real exchange rate adjustment might have caused greater variability in real GDP. Similarly, Imai [8] argues that the dollar peg has failed to deliver price stability to Hong Kong, which experienced high inflation of 7.4% in 1985–1997 before the Asian episode and an extended deflation of - 2.0% in 1998–2007 after the turmoil. While these observations could be valid, in general, higher price inflation in Hong Kong can be attributed to credit expansion by the fractional-reserve banking system that fuels housing and stock market bubbles amidst other domestic circumstances.

In the currency board literature, there is the infamous case of the 2002 collapse of the currency board of Argentina. Cited causes behind the failure include the incapability of the Argentine central bank, the Banco Central de la República Argentina (BCRA), to employ a domestic monetary policy and the overvaluation of the Argentine peso's one-to-one exchange rate with the US dollar [see, e.g., 9].

Against this backdrop, in the wake of the prolonged quantitative easing by the US Federal Reserve, which could have produced huge consequences for the Hong Kong economy, it is appealing to find out how similar or different the circumstances faced by today's Hong Kong are compared to those of Argentina that led to the abandonment of its dollar-linked regime in 2002. In a nutshell, this paper compares Hong Kong in the 2000–2016 period to Argentina in the 1991–2001 period, the lifetime of Argentina's convertibility system. While existing literature often analyzes Hong Kong's currency board in isolation or contrasts it with floating regimes, few studies systematically juxtapose its performance against the specific failure mechanics of the Argentine convertibility system using a unified quantitative framework. This chapter fills this research gap by rigorously testing the orthodox currency board mechanics and optimum currency area (OCA) suitability across both regimes. Theoretically, this contributes to the debate on "corner solutions" in exchange rate regimes by isolating the specific macroeconomic fundamentals, beyond mere political will, that differentiate a sustainable peg from a collapsing one. Dimensions inspected include adherence to currency board principles, macroeconomic performance related to the fixed exchange rate, and compliance with the criteria motivated by the OCA theory. The findings shall indicate the long-run sustainability of the Hong Kong currency board system. Guiding the analysis, the following questions are posed:

(1) How similar are Hong Kong and Argentina in terms of adherence to currency board principles?

(2) How comparable are Hong Kong and Argentina in their macroeconomic performance relevant to a fixed exchange rate regime?

(3) How parallel are Hong Kong and Argentina with respect to conformity to OCA-motivated criteria?

Throughout the analysis, data sampled are constrained by availability but generally range from 2000 to 2016 for Hong Kong and 1991–2001 for Argentina. The rest of the chapter is organized as follows. The second section looks at adherence to currency board principles. Section 3 reviews the macroeconomic performance aspects relevant to exchange rate fixity. The fourth section introduces the OCA theory criteria and evaluates conformity to those criteria. Section 5 discusses possible implications of the findings. Lastly, Section 6 concludes.

The investigation of heterogeneous periods in financial time series requires a disaggregated analysis of indicators rather than reliance on conventional Gaussian-based financial models, as the periods under examination typically constitute atypical or minority regimes relative to normal market conditions [10–12]. This comparative analysis relies on macroeconomic indicators sourced from the IMF International Financial Statistics (IFS) and the World Bank World Development Indicators (WDI). The methodological framework consists of three core components:

(1) Time-period selection

The observation periods were selected to capture critical stress tests for both regimes. For Argentina, the period 1991–2001 is utilized to encompass the Convertibility Plan from its inception through the Tequila Crisis up to its collapse. For Hong Kong, the period 2000–2016 is selected to analyze the board's resilience during and after the 2008 Global Financial Crisis.

(2) Indicators construction

To assess the strict orthodoxy of the currency boards, we calculate the Reserve Pass-through Coefficient. This is defined as the ratio of the change in the monetary base ΔMB to the change in net international reserves ΔNIR.

$$Pass\ Through_t = \Delta MB_t / \Delta NIR_t$$

A coefficient close to 100% indicates strict adherence to orthodox currency board operations. Additionally, external competitiveness is measured using the real exchange rate (RER), deflated by relative consumer price indices (CPI), where an increase denotes appreciation.

(3) To separate long-term structural trends from short-term cyclical fluctuations in GDP and inflation, the Hodrick-Prescott (HP) filter is employed; see, for example, [13, 14]. The operationalization of the HP filter is expressed in the following [15]:

$$Y_t = T_t + C_t \tag{1}$$

Where the original time series (Yt) is decomposed into a trend component (Tt) and a cyclical component (Ct).

$$MIN_T\left\{\sum_{t=1}^{T}(Y_t - T_t)^2 + \lambda\sum_{t=2}^{T-1}[(T_{t+1} - T_t) - (T_t - T_{t-1})]^2\right\} \tag{2}$$

where λ is the smoothing parameter, and λ = 100, 1600, and 14,400 are commonly used for yearly, quarterly, and monthly data, respectively.

2. Adherence to currency board principles

2.1 Net foreign reserves and reserve pass-through

According to [16], a currency board is a monetary authority that issues notes and coins, which are convertible on demand into a foreign anchor currency at a fixed rate of exchange. As reserves, the currency board holds low-risk, interest-bearing bonds denominated in that anchor currency and typically some gold. The reserve levels are set by law and are equal to 100%, or slightly more, of the monetary liabilities (notes, coins, and, if permitted, deposits). By design, a currency board has no discretionary monetary powers and cannot engage in the fiduciary issue of money. Its operations are passive and automatic. Consequently, the quantity of domestic currency in circulation is determined solely by market forces, primarily the demand for domestic currency.

In this regard, Hanke Steve [17] demonstrates a straightforward way to determine, using publicly available data, whether a monetary authority is a pure currency board or a currency-board-like system. For a currency board, net foreign reserves (foreign assets minus foreign liabilities) should be close to 100% of the monetary base (also called reserve money). In addition, "reserve pass-through" (the change in the monetary base divided by the change in net foreign reserves over the period in question) should also be close to 100%. The reserve pass-through is the extent to which changes in net foreign reserves correspond to changes in the monetary base.

Reserve pass-through above 100% means that the monetary base and net foreign reserves change in the same direction, but the monetary base changes more than the net foreign reserves. Reserve pass-through between 0% and 100% means that the monetary base changes less than the net foreign reserves (also called "ordinary sterilization/neutralization"), even though they still move in the same direction. Lastly, reserve pass-through below 0% means that the monetary base and net foreign reserves change in opposite directions (also called "super-sterilization").

Both at 100% and at 0%, no sterilization occurs. A currency board with a fixed exchange rate has reserve pass-through close to 100% because the monetary base changes passively in response to changes in the public's desired holdings of base money, which occur through exchanging the notes, coins, or deposits of the currency board for the anchor currency and vice versa at the fixed exchange rate the board maintains. A central bank with a clean floating exchange rate has a reserve pass-through often close to 0% because it rarely has any reason to buy or sell its currency for foreign reserves.

For each ratio, the closer the value is to 100%, the closer the monetary system will be to the "orthodox" currency board regime. Reserve pass-through of 100% means no sterilization takes place. Specifically, when there are additional money inflows into the domestic economy, the funds are allowed to accumulate as additional reserves held by banks. The monetary authority or central bank does not neutralize the inflows by purchasing assets in foreign currency. Additional reserves in the domestic banking system will hence fuel credit expansion and raise domestic prices. When prices rise, exports of goods and services will decline, reversing the initial money inflows into the economy. Ultimately, the automatic specie flow will bring the external account into balance. In this case, the price of goods and services is the mechanism that equilibrates markets when the price of domestic money in terms of a foreign currency, that is, the exchange rate, is fixed.

The ratios for 1991–2001 Argentina and 2000–16 Hong Kong are presented, respectively, in **Figures 1** and **2**. As **Figure 1** shows, Argentina dramatically deviates from the orthodoxy criteria during its convertibility period. Through the first half and toward the end of its currency board era, which makes up most of the period shown, its net foreign reserves are insufficient to cover all its monetary liabilities. In addition, as signified by its reserve pass-through ratio, over almost the whole period, Argentina has been engaging in monetary sterilizations, where a substantial number of sterilizations are super-sterilizations.

On the contrary, as **Figure 2** portrays, Hong Kong's net foreign reserves ratio is always greater than 100%, though the figure has decreased remarkably, from an

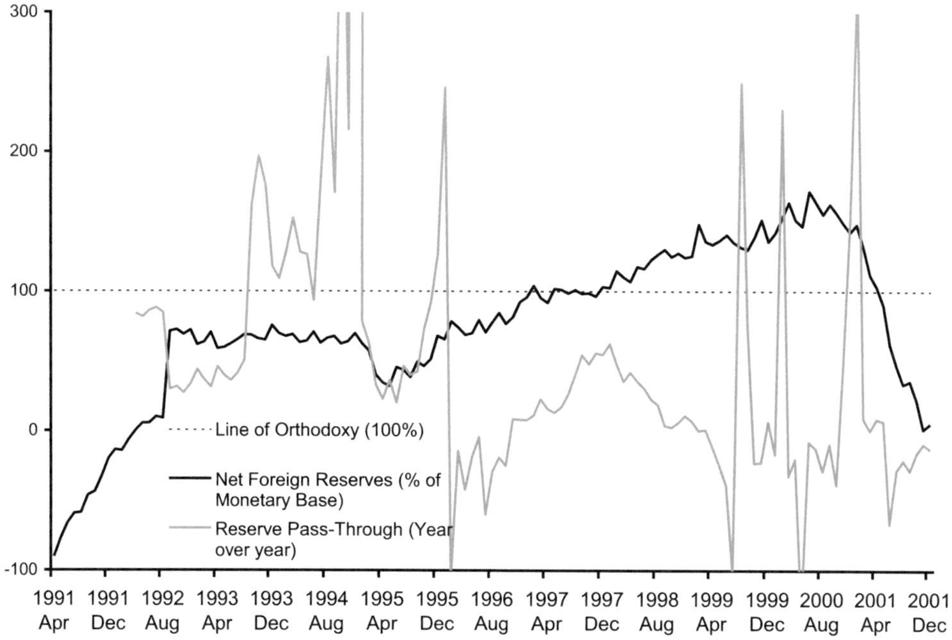

Figure 1.
Currency board orthodoxy measures, Argentina, 1991:4–2001:12 (source: computed from IMF data).

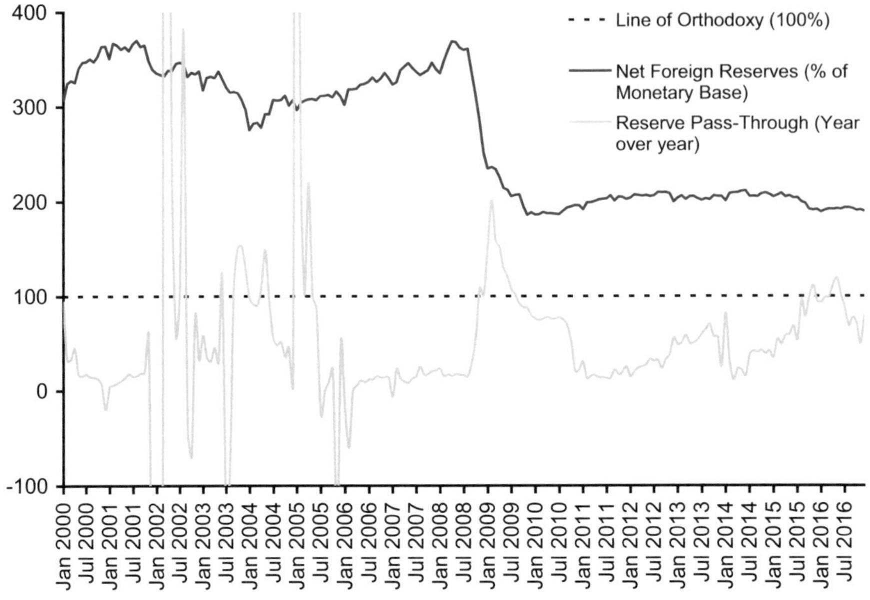

Figure 2.
Currency board orthodoxy measures, Hong Kong, 2000:1–2016:12. (source: computed from IMF data).

average of 300% to around 200% since the 2008 financial crisis. The decline is consistent with the credit crunch and severe economic downturn affecting Hong Kong during that time. On neutralization, even though the Hong Kong Monetary Authority (HKMA) does engage in sterilizations, as indicated by deviations of its reserve pass-through, most of the time the sterilizations are ordinary sterilizations as opposed to Argentina's super-sterilizations. Meantime, the great gyrations in reserve pass-through in the early years of 2000 leading to the subprime crisis can be attributed to the prolonged monetary easing of the US Federal Reserve following the dot-com crash and the September 11 attacks. On this finding, the HKMA appears to have engaged in sterilizations to curb over-heating in the asset markets.

To summarize, both Argentina and Hong Kong do deviate from the currency board principles, but in comparison, that of 2000–2016 Hong Kong is clearly less severe than that of 1991–2001 Argentina. Ever since the asset boom and the great recession of 2008–2009, the reserve pass-through of Hong Kong has been between 0% and 100%, indicating that both net foreign reserves and the monetary base move in the same direction but to different extents. Probably, this "maneuver" of the monetary base is an attempt to manipulate the money supply and price level since the base money is the reserve over which fractional-reserve banks expand their demand deposits and other liabilities to depositors. The effectiveness of the HKMA to effect change in the money supply and price inflation, of course, still depends on the balance sheets of commercial banks.

2.2 Convergence of nominal interest rate with anchor country

Under a strict fixed exchange rate regime, such as a pure currency board system, the domestic nominal interest rate should run in parallel with that of the anchor country. This is so because the nominal exchange rate against the anchor currency is assumed to be constantly fixed, and in the presence of free flow of financial capital with the anchor country, any interest rate differentials with the anchor country will be quickly eliminated by arbitraging transactions through the money markets. Of course, due to transaction costs, risk perceptions, and money demand conditions, small short-run differentials between the rates are not uncommon, even for bonds of the same terms to maturity.

Along these lines, it is instructive to examine how parallel the money market rates in Argentina and Hong Kong are with those in the United States. From **Figure 3**, it is apparent that the Argentine money market rate deviates substantially from the US rate over the entire period, and the periods of large deviations do match the periods of deviation of the reserve pass-through ratio seen in the previous section. This is not surprising since discretionary monetary policy in Argentina, as indicated by sharp deviations of its reserve pass-through from 100%, coupled with relatively low levels of net foreign reserve coverage, should have undermined market confidence in the peso-dollar currency board regime. Accordingly, due to downward expectations of the peso against the dollar, lenders would require an exchange risk premium, as indicated by the much higher nominal interest rates through down-bidding the price of peso-denominated bonds. Hence, through 1991–2001, as **Figure 3** plainly reveals, the money market rate of Argentina is consistently above that of the United States.

Quite differently, consistent with its credible fixed dollar regime, during 2000–16, Hong Kong's money market rate virtually moved in tandem with the US one, showing only slight deviations from the US rate (note that **Figure 3** uses a significantly smaller vertical scale for interest rates for Hong Kong than for Argentina). Notably, the immediate impact of Lehman's collapse on Hong Kong's interest rate can be seen in the sharp spike in the money market rate in September 2008, following diminished confidence in lending. The stress was largely caused by the abrupt repatriation of dollars back to the US markets following the credit crunch in the United States and Europe [18].

In sum, probably due to the lack of credibility of its fixed exchange rate regime, the nominal money market rate of Argentina in 1991–2001 is always greater than the US rate. Quite the opposite, due to sufficient credibility as demonstrated by the more-than-ample foreign reserves, the money market rate of Hong Kong is virtually symmetrical with the US rate.

3. Macroeconomic performance

3.1 Real exchange rate and international competitiveness

The exceptionally greater Argentine interest rate than the American rate in 2000–2001, as shown in **Figure 3**, reflects the downward expectation of the peso against the dollar and heightened uncertainty in the Argentine banking system (see, e.g., [9]). On top of that, the money supply in Argentina, as measured by M2, had also been falling in 1998–2001, as made clear in **Figure 4** (data range constrained by data availability). The drastic collapse of M2 in 2000 indicates a drastic fall in bank credit and deposit creation, which is consistent with the diminishing nominal GDP and decreasing consumer price level, as given in the same figure.

On the other hand, Hong Kong's M2 in 2001–16 has been rising increasingly more rapidly than its nominal GDP, consistent with its rising consumer prices. Nevertheless, huge price inflation in properties and stocks, which is common in this densely-populated small territory, is not captured by the CPI. This upward trend of

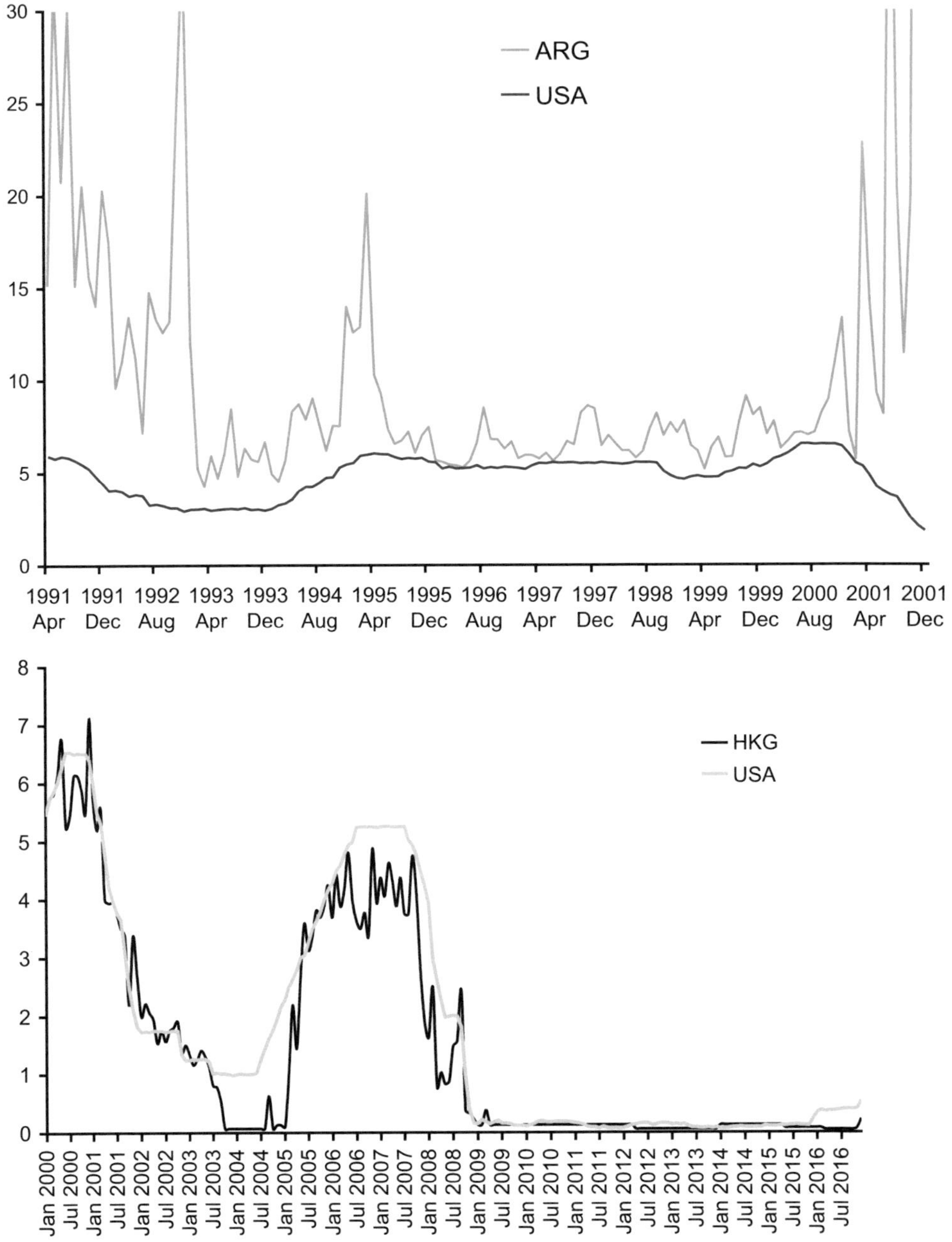

Figure 3.
Money market rate (%), Argentina 1991:4–2001:12; Hong Kong 2000:1–2016:12. (source: computed from IMF data).

price levels in Hong Kong corroborates with multiple rounds of monetary easing by the Federal Reserve since the subprime crisis and flows of hot money into the Hong Kong markets despite the ordinary sterilizations undertaken by the currency board. While increases in base money within the banking system can be slowed

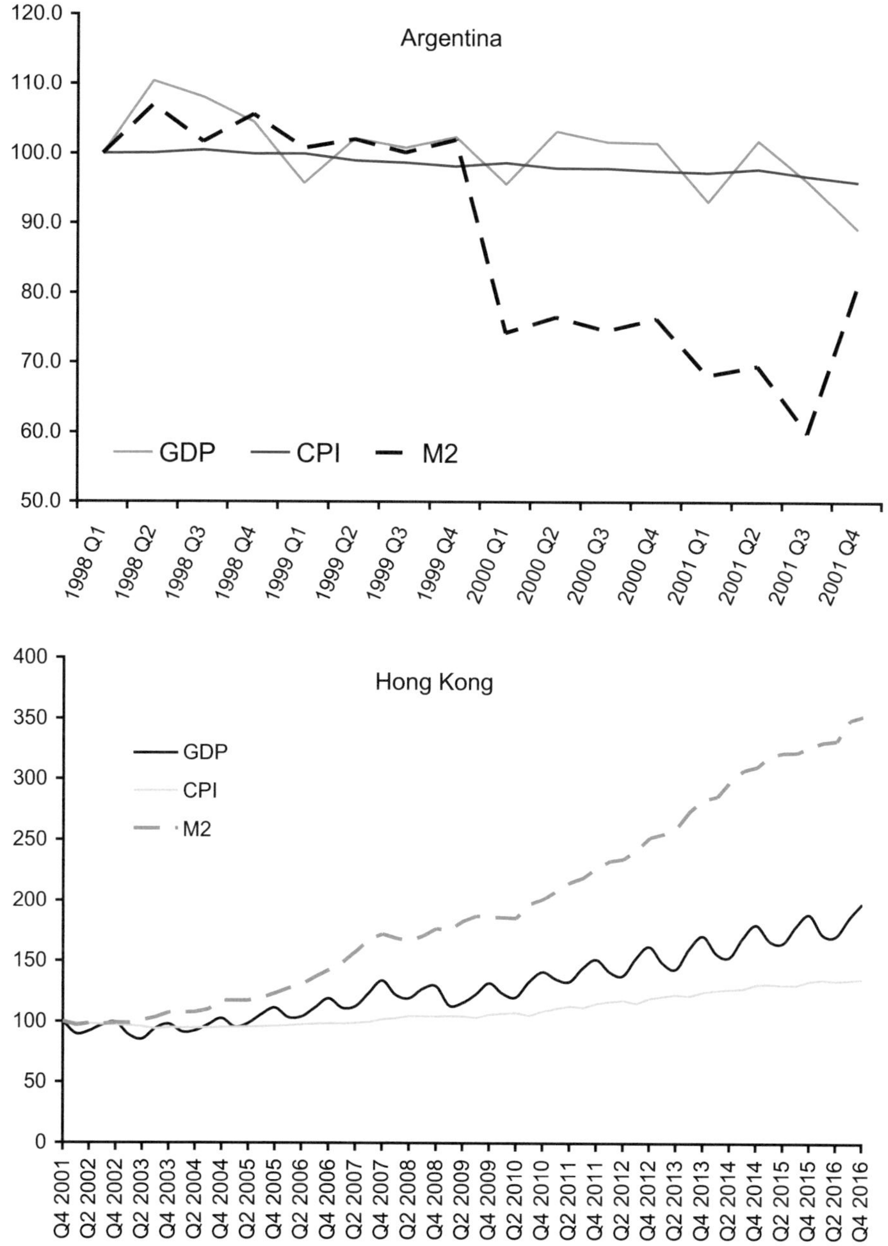

Figure 4.
Nominal GDP, CPI, and M2, Argentina 1998:Q1–2001:Q4; Hong Kong 2001:Q4–2016:Q4. Note: adequate data for Argentina is not available for the earlier time period (source: computed from IMF data).

down through sterilizations, price inflation can be easily fueled by deposit creation, as indicated by the fast-growing M2.

The above explains the falling price trend in 1998–2001 Argentina and the rising price trend in 2001–2016 Hong Kong. Since the nominal exchange rate is fixed, checking the price trend is essential when evaluating trade competitiveness. Normally, the trajectory of a country's nominal exchange rate against the dollar is critical when assessing the price competitiveness of exports, particularly in the short run when changes in relative prices are sticky. In 1991–2001, hence, since the official exchange rate of the Argentine peso against the dollar had been practically stable, it is useful to look at the path of the real exchange rate as one way of gauging export competitiveness.

Figure 5 clearly shows that the peso was depreciating against the dollar in real terms (real exchange rate deflated by relative CPI) from the mid-1990s to 2001, even though the peso had been appreciating in real terms in the early 1990s. The falling real exchange rate in the later period could have helped Argentina's export sector. This is particularly relevant in tourism, which can be directly boosted by a relatively low consumer price level. Quantitatively, the divergence is distinct – Argentina experienced a rigid appreciation in real terms prior to the final years of the regime, whereas Hong Kong demonstrated necessary flexibility. The data suggest that Hong Kong's internal price adjustments allowed for a corrective depreciation in the RER index during the post-crisis period, empirically validating the internal devaluation mechanism required for regime survival, in contrast to Argentina's prolonged overvaluation.

For Hong Kong, the Hong Kong dollar was no longer depreciating against the dollar in real terms from the mid-2000s through 2016; in fact, it was appreciating, and this reverse track can be attributed to the greater pace of CPI inflation in Hong Kong. As a general rule, though its nominal dollar rate is stable, Hong Kong is still susceptible to inflationary pressure from the influx of short-term financial capital so that, if the inflation is transmitted to its export sector, it can raise the Hong Kong dollar in real terms and undermine trade competitiveness.

Based on the findings above, in the run-up period to the breakdown of its currency board regime, Argentina might have gained in mercantile competitiveness with respect to lower prices if the prices of exports somehow moved in tandem with consumer prices. As for Hong Kong, since the mid-2000s, this small open economy has no longer enjoyed rising competitiveness through real depreciation. Instead, its goods and services have become increasingly expensive in terms of the US dollar.

3.2 External balance

Balance of payments can be important in maintaining public confidence and, hence, the sustainability of a fixed exchange rate regime, such as a currency board-like system, especially when foreign reserves are inadequate in covering the money supply in local currency. The public may look at the current account balance, of which a current account surplus indicates earnings of foreign currency that are essential in servicing debt in foreign currency. Part of this earned foreign income will be held as reserves by banks and monetary authorities. A persistent current account deficit for a developing country with a soft currency and huge foreign debt servicing can be alarming, as the country can default on servicing and repayment of the principal owed to foreigners. Meantime, the total stock of borrowing or liabilities owed to foreigners is accounted for by the net international investment position. If the central bank or currency board does not have sufficient foreign reserves to redeem money and deposits in local currency, a run on the local currency can occur, and this can collapse convertibility and the currency board regime.

Figure 6 shows the key components of the balance of payments and the international investment position of Argentina. Notably, Argentina consistently recorded a current account deficit from 1992 to 2001, and this deficit was largely

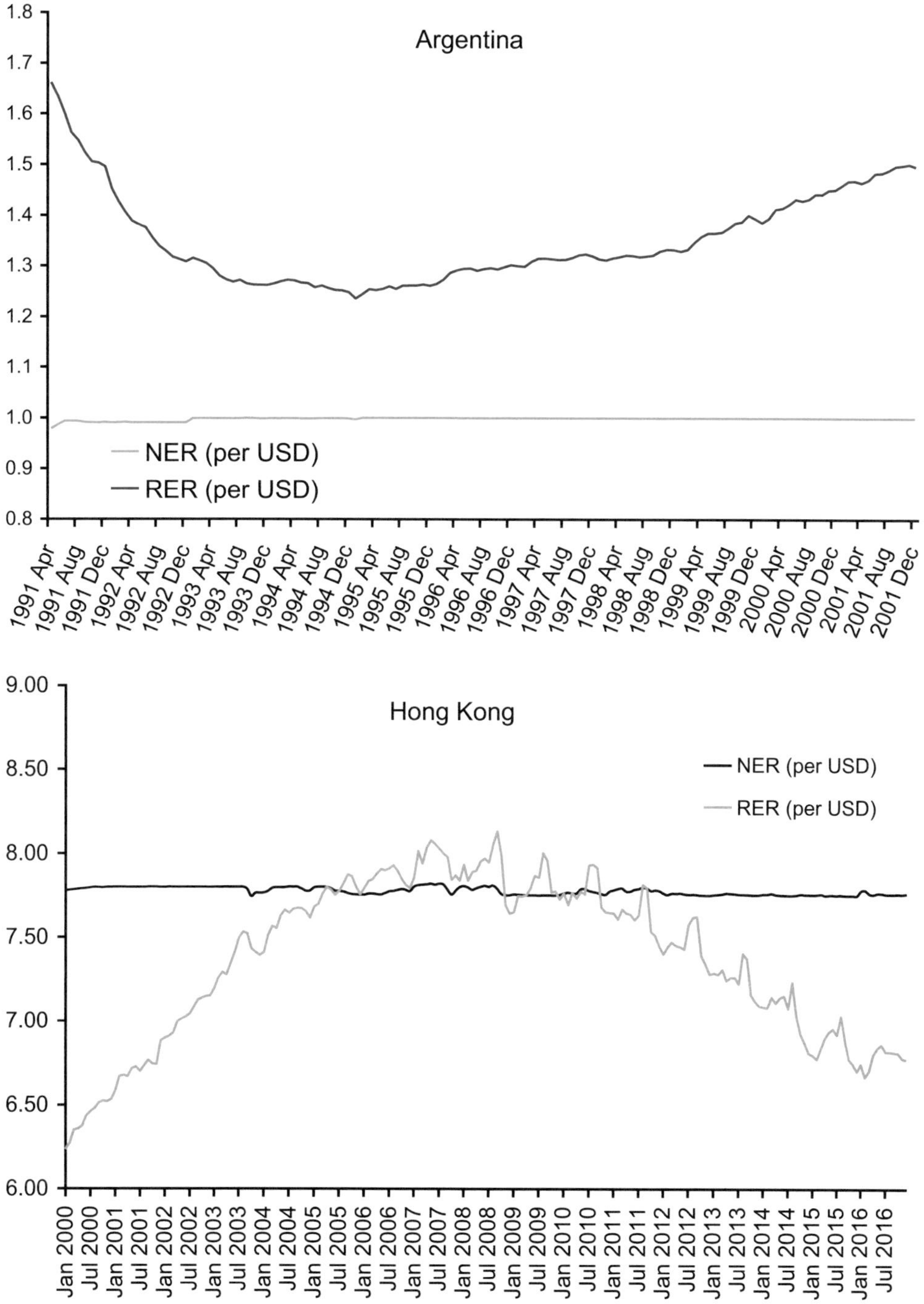

Figure 5.
Nominal and real dollar rates (deflated by relative CPI), Argentina 1991:4–2001:12; Hong Kong 2000: 1–2016:12 (source: computed from IMF data).

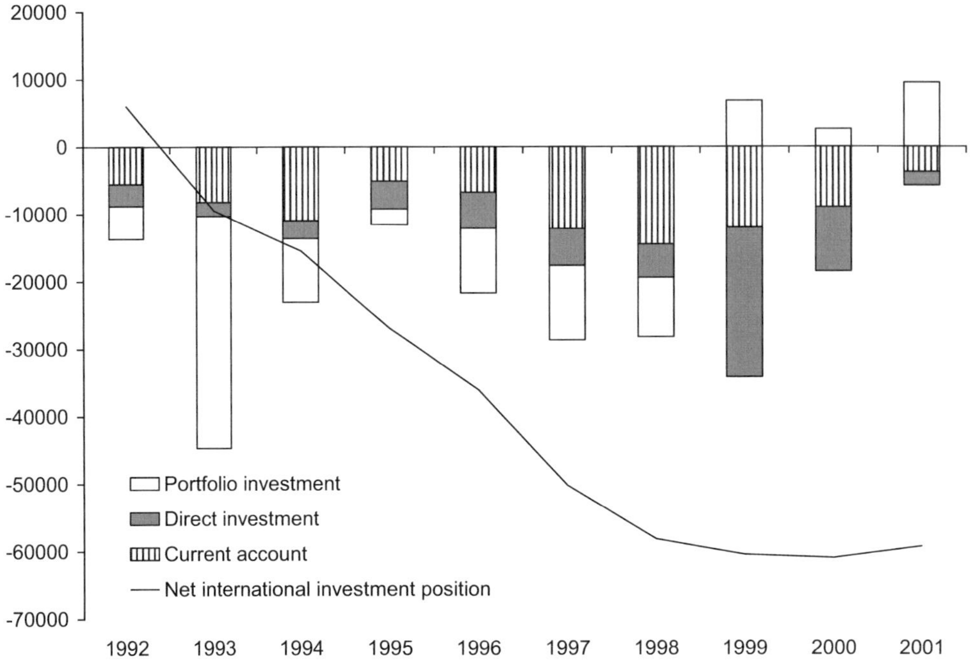

Figure 6.
Balance of payments and international investment position (US$ m), Argentina, 1992–2001 (source: computed from IMF-balance-of-payments data).

financed by net increases in liabilities to foreigners, as shown by negative values in portfolio investment (until 1998) and direct investment, along with the corresponding decline in the net international investment position. While direct investment from abroad is constructive and contributes to production and employment, portfolio investment funds from abroad can be speculative and destructive when the funds leave the country. Huge hot money flows into the Argentine financial market were observed in 1993 amid a short boom following an attempt to curtail hyperinflation by the Argentine government through the peso-dollar peg. Despite the above, conditions improved in 1999–2001 with remarkable foreign direct investment, net increases in portfolio asset holdings abroad, a diminishing current account deficit, and hence leveling off of the negative net international investment position. This could be the result of measures to boost inward FDIs, namely measures such as trade and capital account liberalizations, privatization programs, and deregulations by the government.

Quite the opposite, as **Figure** 7 exhibits, from 2001 to 2016, Hong Kong has always enjoyed a current account surplus. Also, except for the year 2000, there have been consistent net portfolio investment outflows from this international financial hub. Together with its rising international creditor status, this demonstrates increasing holdings of net foreign assets by Hong Kong-based institutions and individuals.

In a nutshell, pertaining to external balance, the 1992–2001 Argentina suffered a persistent current account deficit that was financed principally by foreign liabilities. As a result of massive capital flight amidst a public debt crisis, convertibility was ended, and Argentina's peg to the dollar had to be abandoned. On the contrary, the 2000–2016 Hong Kong demonstrated a persistent current account surplus and rising

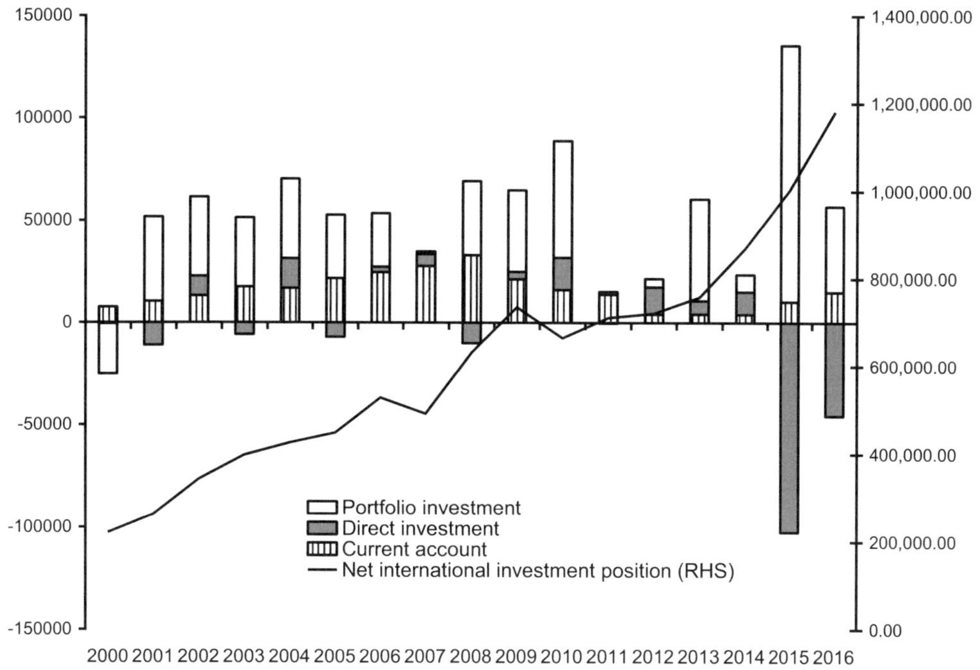

Figure 7.
Balance of Payments and International Investment Position (US$ m), Hong Kong, 2000–2016. Note: RHS = right-hand side scale (source: computed from IMF-balance-of-payments data).

net creditorship with the rest of the world, which were essential to market confidence in its dollar-linked currency board system.

3.3 Real growth and price inflation

Demand for money derives from its purchasing power on goods and services. For this reason, ceteris paribus, the greater the output growth of a country, the greater the demand for its currency. Hence, the greater the output growth of a currency board economy, the less likely the redemption into the base money or the anchor currency (i. e., the dollar for Argentina and Hong Kong), the stronger will be the currency board system. Similarly, since purchasing power is a function of price inflation, the lower the price inflation of the purchasable goods, the greater the purchasing power of the corresponding currency, the greater the demand for it, the less likely is the redemption into the base money or the switch into other assets or monies.

Table 1 shows real growth and price inflation for 1991–2001 in Argentina and 2000–16 in Hong Kong. In terms of real GDP growth, Argentina experienced four years of negative growth at - 2.85%, - 3.39%, - 0.79%, and - 4.41% in 1995, 1999, 2000, and 2001, respectively, whereas Hong Kong only experienced one year of negative growth at - 2.66% in 2009 during the great recession following the US subprime bust.

With respect to inflation, Argentina successfully curbed its hyperinflation in the early 1990s and maintained low single-digit inflation until the final years of its convertibility regime, when it experienced deflation. On the contrary, Hong Kong experienced deflation in the early 2000s and low to moderate inflation thereafter.

		Real GDP growth (%)		CPI inflation (%)		GDP deflator inflation (%)	
ARG	HKG	ARG	HKG	ARG	HKG	ARG	HKG
1991	2000	12.67	7.66	171.67	-3.69	132.95	-3.39
1992	2001	11.94	0.56	24.90	-1.66	11.92	-1.77
1993	2002	5.91	1.66	10.61	-2.98	-1.47	-3.40
1994	2003	5.84	3.06	4.18	-2.67	2.85	-6.01
1995	2004	-2.85	8.70	3.38	-0.27	3.17	-3.59
1996	2005	5.53	7.39	0.16	0.83	-0.05	-0.15
1997	2006	8.11	7.03	0.53	2.05	-0.46	-0.53
1998	2007	3.85	6.46	0.92	2.01	-1.71	3.14
1999	2008	-3.39	2.13	-1.17	4.33	-1.84	1.28
2000	2009	-0.79	-2.46	-0.94	0.63	1.04	-0.38
2001	2010	-4.41	6.77	-1.07	2.25	-1.10	0.27
	2011		4.81		5.26		3.90
	2012		1.70		4.07		3.54
	2013		3.10		4.35		1.81
	2014		2.76		4.49		2.85
	2015		2.39		2.97		3.64
	2016		2.05		2.39		1.78

Source: World Bank: WDI.

Table 1.
Real growth and price inflation: Argentina, 1991–2001; Hong Kong, 2000–2016.

Similar observations can be seen when the broader price index, the GDP deflator, is used to indicate inflation.

To summarize, from 2000 to 2016, Hong Kong enjoyed stable economic growth and price inflation, which could bolster its currency board regime, in contrast to the unstable 1991–2001 period in Argentina.

4. Optimum currency area criteria

The foundations of OCA theory are laid out by [19, 20], and subsequently refined by [21, 22]. In essence, the OCA theory outlines the criteria under which a monetary and economic area can reap the most benefits while, at the same time, minimizing the costs of fixing the exchange rate with another monetary area.

In a nutshell, the OCA theory relates to the benefits and costs of exchange rate fixity, which rely on the extent of convergence between the economies. The gains include reduction in transaction and information costs, enhanced certainty in economic calculations, improved efficiency of the price mechanism and allocation of resources, and greater credibility of the monetary authority. On the drawbacks, they are fundamentally the costs of relinquishing self-governing monetary and exchange rate tools that can be helpful in buffering transitory economic shocks.

In the spirit of OCA theory, we shall compare Hong Kong with Argentina in respect to the appropriateness of fixing the dollar rate. Following [23, 24], the OCA criteria investigated are bilateral trade intensity, business cycle symmetry, inflation convergence, and real interest rate synchronization. For these four dimensions, the degree of conformity to the theory is dependent on a reference country; in the present case, the reference is the United States. These criteria have been implemented earlier by [13], whose efficacy is evidenced when Portugal, Italy, Greece, and Spain are singled out as the ones with the least conforming OCA features.

4.1 Trade openness and bilateral trade intensity

As asserted by [19, 20], the greater the openness of an economy to trade, the greater the desirability of fixing the exchange rate with a common medium of exchange. Besides the benefits of certainty and transaction cost savings, fixed exchange rates could also stabilize domestic prices. This is so because, for a highly open economy, depreciation or appreciation of the national currency is detrimental to the economy. Depreciation raises the prices of imports and locally produced substitutes for imports, reducing the purchasing power of money. Appreciation raises the prices of exports and lowers the prices of imports and local import substitutes, leading to unemployment. Disruption is greater if movement in the exchange rate is unrelated to changes in the demand and supply of real goods and services. Hence, countries that achieve the greatest levels of bilateral trade also experience the greatest increase in readiness for monetary unification [25].

Along these lines, it is compelling to examine trade openness of Argentina in 1991–2001 and that of Hong Kong in 2001–2016. To measure this dimension, the percentage of trade of goods and services over GDP is used. In addition to this, it is also crucial to check if the US has been appropriate as the monetary anchor country for Argentina and Hong Kong. This is done by looking at their trade intensities with the United States. To quantify the extent of trade openness with the United States, a bilateral trade intensity measure is used. For Argentina or Hong Kong, denoted as i, trade openness with the United States is measured by bilateral trade intensity, $(x_{i,r} + m_{i,r})/(x_i + m_i)$ where x_i and m_i are the exports and imports of goods of Argentina or Hong Kong and subscript r indicates destination to or source from the US.

As **Figure 8** shows, the general trade openness of Argentina rises during 1991–97 and hovers at about 20–25% of GDP until 2001. Over the whole period examined, an apparent downfall in openness can be seen in 1999, the year marking the Brazilian currency crisis. For Hong Kong, trade openness has always been above 250% of GDP, along with a long-run uptrend. Despite this, a significant drop can be seen in 2009 during the global recession. With the United States, Hong Kong's trade in goods and services experiences a downward trend.

In short, findings suggest that, with respect to trade, 1991–2001 Argentina was a relatively closed economy when compared to 2001–2016 Hong Kong. Hence, since the US dollar has always been and still is the international currency, Hong Kong should have gained more than Argentina did from fixity to the dollar. Even though Hong Kong's bilateral trade with the United States is declining, as long as the dollar remains the world's dominant finance and trade currency, Hong Kong continues to gain tremendously from exchange rate fixation with the dollar because international transactions are, by and large, conducted in dollars.

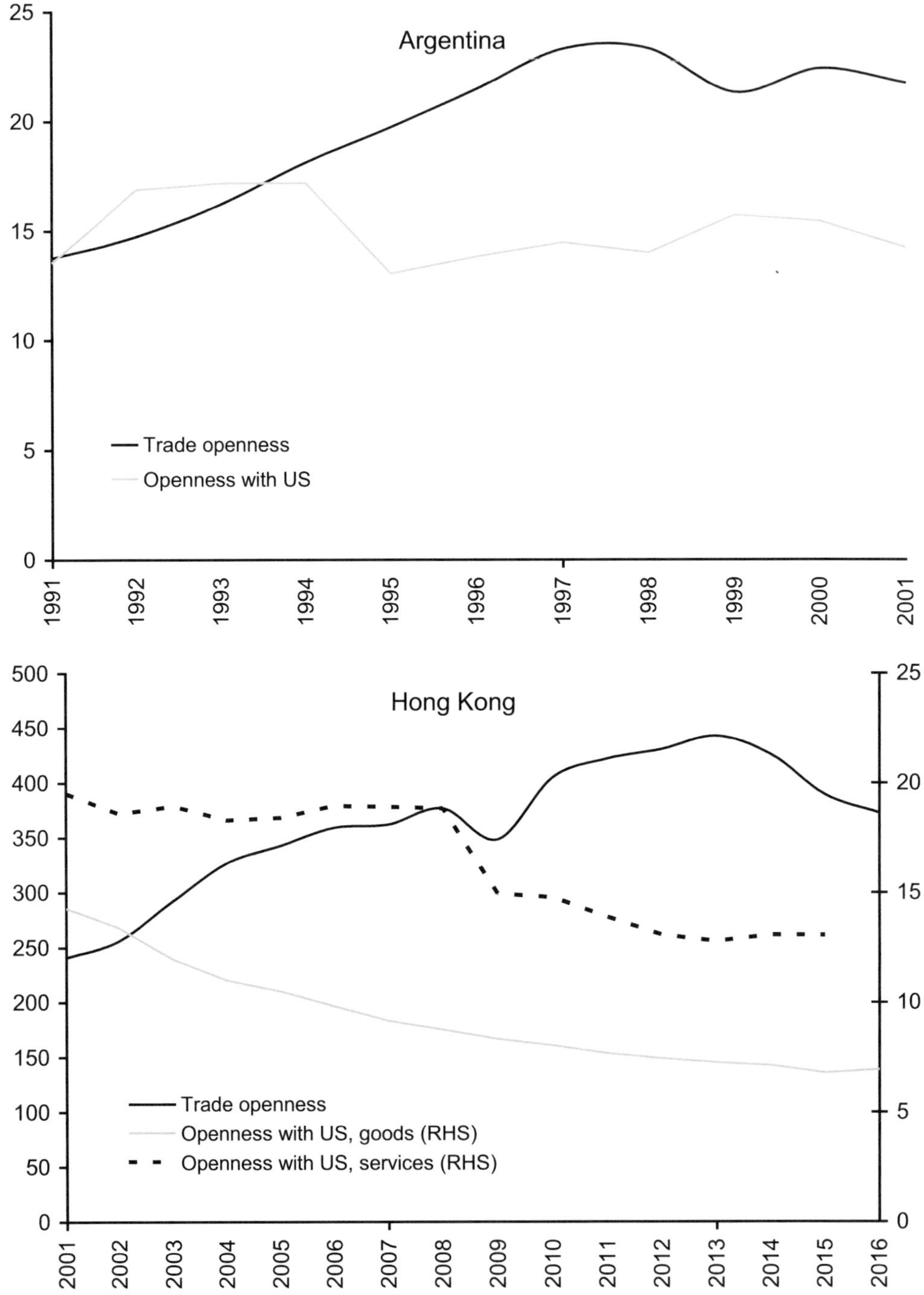

Figure 8.
Trade openness measures (%), Argentina 1991–2001; Hong Kong 2001–2016 (source: IMF: DOTS, World Bank: WDI, International Trade Center: Trade Map).

4.2 Business cycle symmetry

When business cycles are synchronous between two currency areas, the ability of a flexible exchange rate to buffer asymmetric shocks is not only irrelevant but can even be destabilizing. Hence, the greater the business cycle synchronicity with the US, the stronger the case for adopting the US monetary policy and the corresponding fixed dollar rate regime. In terms of quantification, it is common to implement this criterion according to the synchronicity of business cycles by looking at the cyclical component of output. Here, the method of [26, 27] is adopted, where the cyclical component of the annual real GDP series is extracted using the HP filter.

Figure 9 compares the business cycles of 1991–2001 Argentina and 2000–2016 Hong Kong, respectively, with the corresponding US cycle. The standardized values of the cyclical components of output, which signify the business cycles, are scaled on the left axes. The standardized differentials against the United States, which indicate the extent of divergence from the US cycle, are represented on the right axes. From the charts, it is apparent that, with respect to business cycle symmetry, Hong Kong is highly convergent with the United States in comparison to Argentina.

4.3 Inflation convergence

According to [13], the traditional OCA literature originated in the era of "fixed-price" economics; so introducing inflation convergence as one criterion is regarded as a normalization. In another respect, since similar price inflations can result from similarities in monetary and fiscal policies and economic structure, the cost of joining a currency area is presumably low when inflations are similar across members [28]. Besides, convergence in inflation may also reflect similarity in trade union aggressiveness and labor costs, implying lesser need for flexibility in nominal exchange rates in correcting current account imbalances [29].

From **Figure 10**, we can see that inflation in Argentina has fallen significantly since the implementation of the convertibility regime in 1991. Nonetheless, after the remarkable convergence with the United States in the mid-1990s, Argentina began to diverge from the U.S. It even experienced deflation in the run-up years to the collapse of the convertibility system. As for Hong Kong, it had been increasingly convergent with the United States until the 2009 great recession but has somewhat diverged since then. The divergence of Hong Kong, however, is generally small when compared to that of Argentina.

4.4 Real interest rate synchronicity

If the monetary policy of a country has historically differed little from that of the reference country, the cost of relinquishing monetary independence is accordingly low, so that synchronicity in real interest rates may be interpreted as an indicator of coordination in monetary policy [13]. In addition, interest rate synchronicity with a credible country also implies a willingness to commit to a counter-inflationary stance (see, e.g., [30]). Following [13], real interest rate series are detrended by applying the H–P filter, as with the business cycle criterion. To ensure consistency across cases, the lending rate and CPI inflation rate are used to compute the real interest rate.

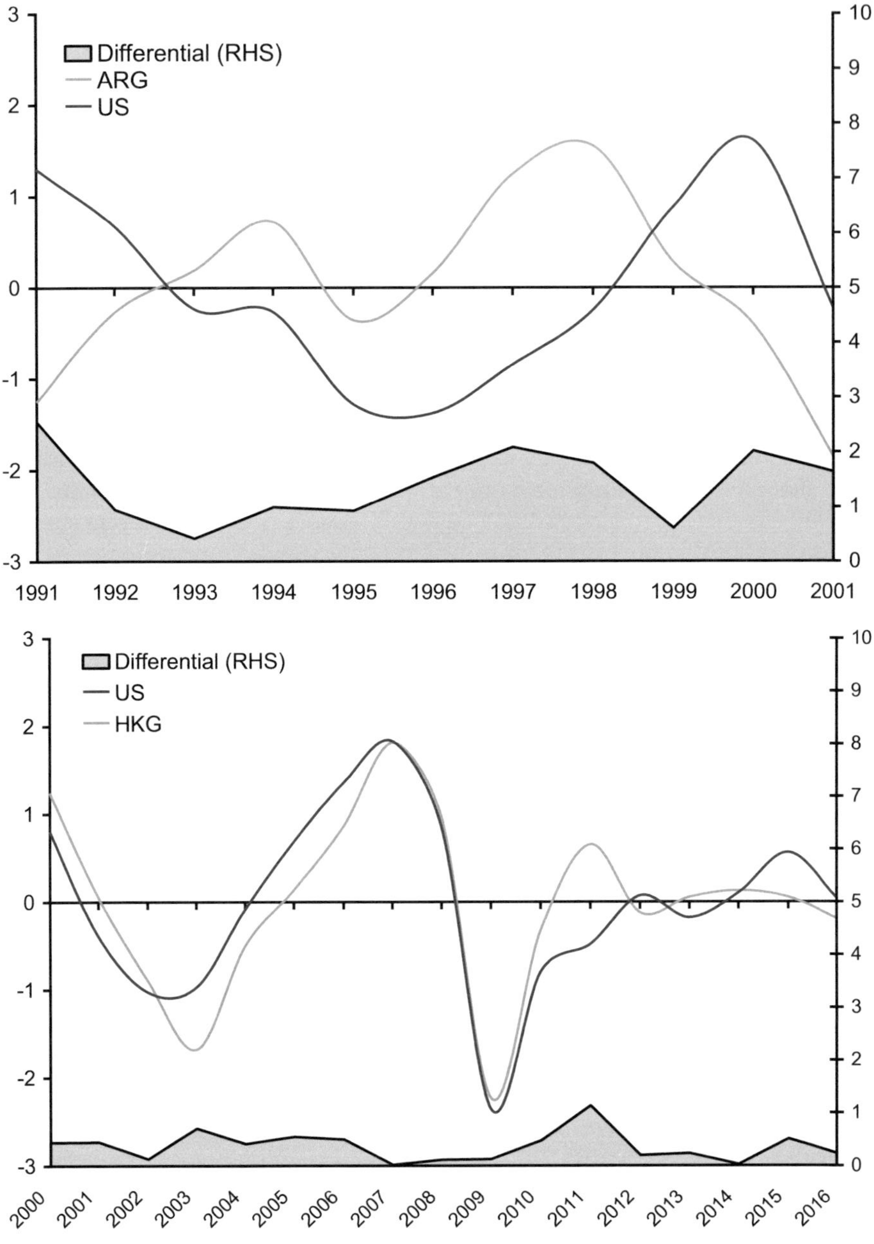

Figure 9.
Comparison with the US business cycle: Argentina 1991–2001; Hong Kong 2000–2016 (source: IMF: IFS).

As depicted in **Figure 11**, the Argentina interest rate path is virtually uncorrelated with the US path. On the other hand, the Hong Kong real interest rate trajectory is essentially in parallel with the US one. When one looks at the differentials quantified by the right vertical axis, it is clear that Argentina's deviations are remarkably greater than Hong Kong's.

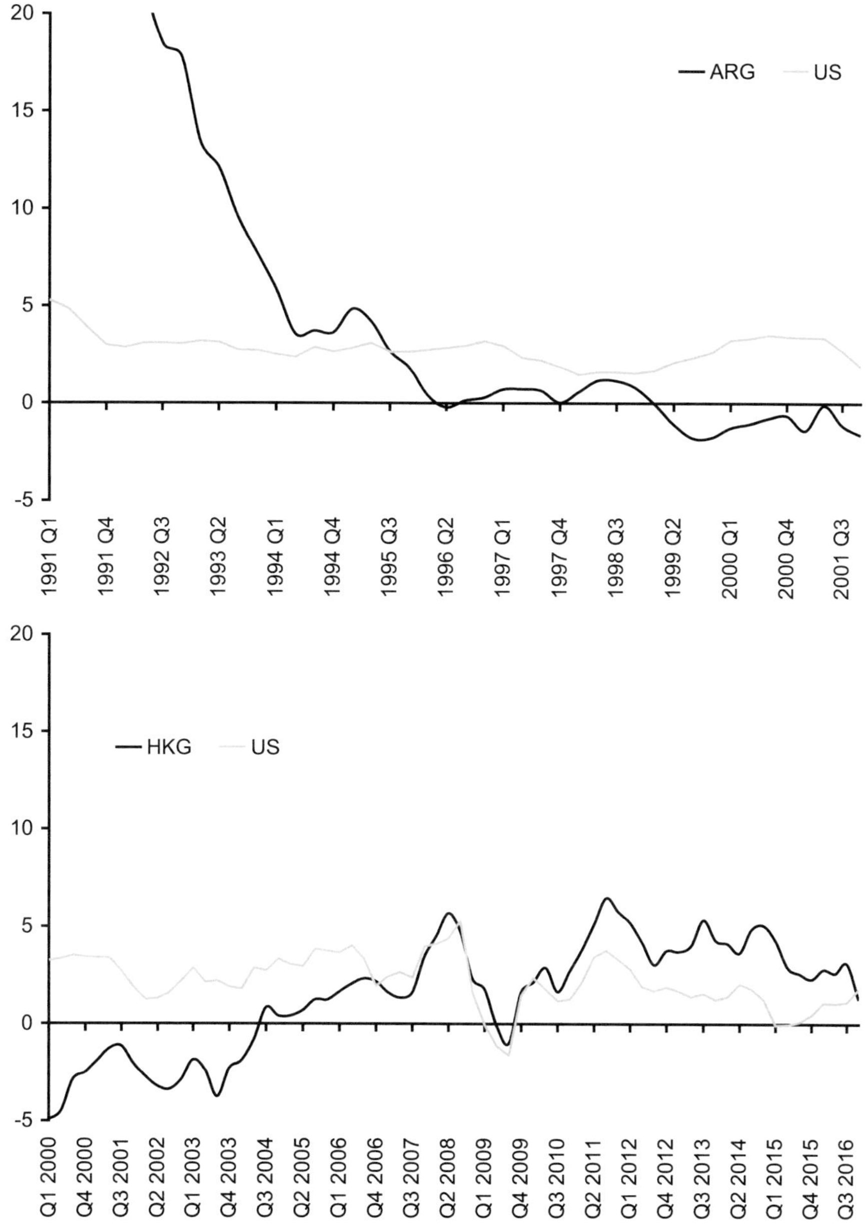

Figure 10.
Comparison with the US CPI inflation: Argentina (1991Q1–2001Q4) and Hong Kong (2000Q1–2016Q4) (source: IMF, IFS).

The evidence suggests that the monetary policy of Argentina has been effectively independent from that of the United States, and this suggests that Argentina has not been running a strict fixed exchange regime. On the contrary, the Hong Kong monetary policy is virtually parallel with the American one.

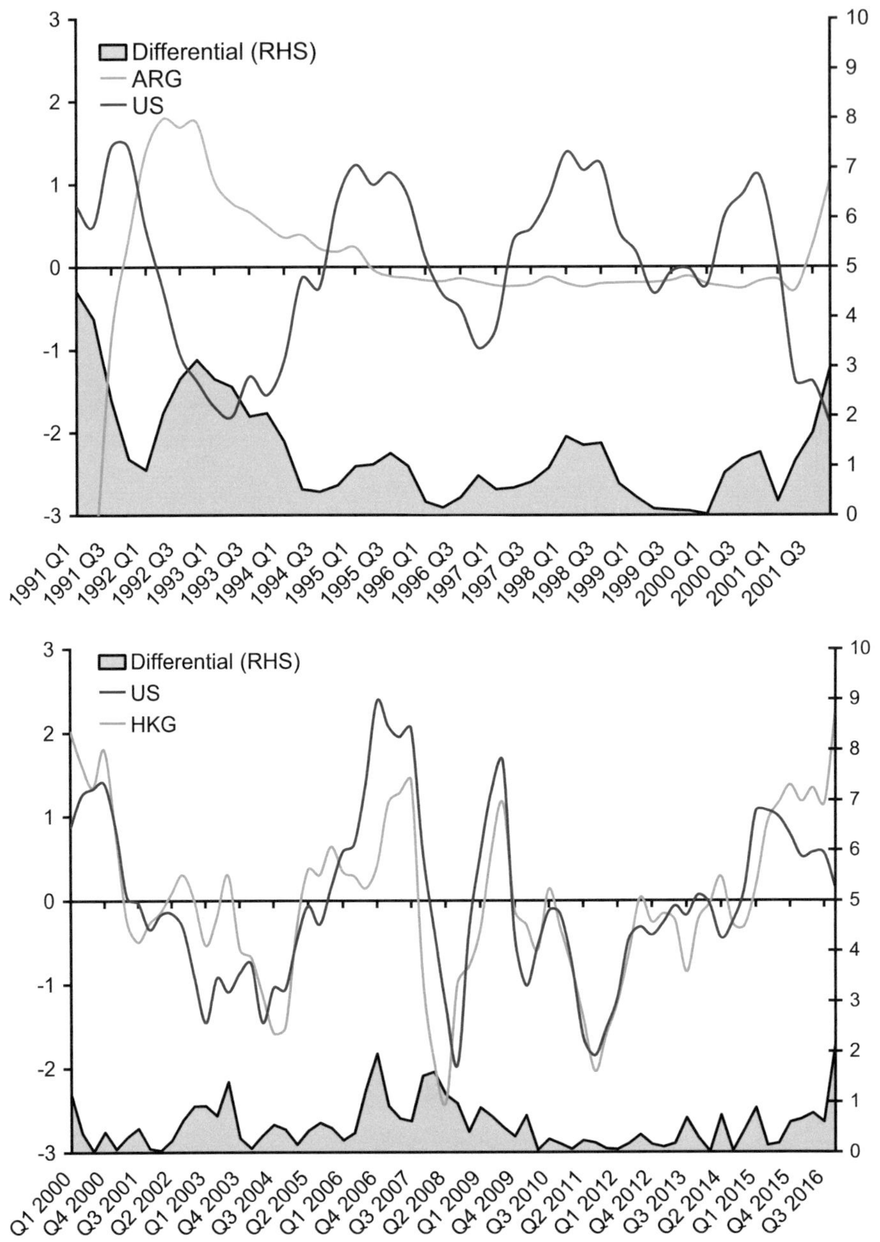

Figure 11.
Comparison with the US real lending rate: Argentina (1991Q1–2001Q4) and Hong Kong (2000Q1–2016Q4) (source: IFS).

5. Discussion

Hitherto, the discussions have examined how similar or different the 2000–2016 Hong Kong is compared to the 1991–2001 Argentina in respect to their adherence to currency board principles, macroeconomic performance, and conformity to optimal currency area criteria. The motivation is such that if the conditions of Hong Kong are substantially close to those of Argentina, the currency board of Hong Kong will be unsustainable. A summary of the findings is provided in **Table 2**.

On adherence to currency board principles, the 2000–2016 Hong Kong is substantively different from the 1991–2001 Argentina. Akin to Argentina, Hong

	Criteria	Argentina in 1991–2001	Hong Kong in 2000–2016
	Currency board principles		
1	Net foreign reserves-to-monetary base ratio (should be 100% for a true currency board).	Most of the time, below 100%.	Always above 100%.
2	Reserve pass-through ratio (should be 100% for a true currency board).	Deviated from 100% most of the time. More "super" sterilizations.	Deviated from 100% most of the time. Fewer "super" sterilizations.
3	Nominal interest rate convergence.	Deviated significantly from the United States.	Significantly convergent with the United States
	Macroeconomic performance		
1	Real exchange rate (RER) and international competitiveness.	RER appreciated, then depreciated. It could have been more competitive with the United States in the later period.	RER depreciated, then appreciated. Could have been less competitive with the United States in the later period.
2	External balance.	Persistent current account deficit that is financed principally by increasing international indebtedness.	Persistent current account surplus and rising international creditorship.
3	Real growth and price inflation.	Relatively unstable growth and price inflation.	Relatively stable growth and price inflation.
	OCA criteria		
1	General trade openness and trade intensity with the United States.	Trade openness has always been less than 25% of GDP. Openness in goods trade with the US is about 15%.	Trade openness has always been above 250% of GDP. Openness in goods trade with the United States is less than 15% and declining. Data for services trade is unavailable, but given Hong Kong's status as an international financial hub, fixation to the dollar is important.
2	Business cycle symmetry.	Noticeably divergent from the United States.	Remarkably convergent with the United States.
3	Convergence in CPI inflation.	Generally more convergent.	Generally more convergent.
4	Real interest rate synchronicity.	Remarkably different from the United States.	Remarkably parallel with the United States.

Table 2.
Summary of findings.

Kong has also undertaken sterilizations – not what an orthodox currency board principle would prescribe. Despite this deviation from orthodoxy, however, market confidence has always been in place due to its abundant foreign reserves. This confidence in the Hong Kong system is manifested in the convergence of money market rates between Hong Kong and the United States.

Apparently, purchases and accumulation of foreign assets by Hong Kong authorities are intended to restrain the growth of domestic money supply and price inflation caused by excessive inflows of financial capital by limiting the reserves that banks hold. Nonetheless, credit expansion by fractional-reserve commercial banks still fuels price inflation, particularly in the stock and housing markets. A better solution would be for the monetary authority to refrain from any sterilization and instead require banks to fully back their Hong Kong dollar-denominated liabilities. Under this approach, the price mechanism can perform its functions of allocation and signaling efficiently and internationally, without distortions and exaggerations created by the credit expansion of fractional-reserve banks.

The second question of research pertains to macroeconomic performance. As a measure of international competitiveness, in the long run, when prices are elastic and when rises in prices are passed-through to the exportable sector, the real dollar exchange rate of Hong Kong indicates diminishing trade competitiveness for Hong Kong. By the same measure, Argentina, on the other hand, gains competitiveness in the preceding years before the abolishment of its currency board. This gain, however, is a result of a falling price level preceded by a decreasing money supply after bank runs. While real depreciation could have, to an extent, helped reduce the current account deficit of Argentina, over the entire period examined, its current account is still in deficit and financed through rising indebtedness. On the contrary, Hong Kong enjoys favorable external balance in addition to stability in growth and price inflation.

The third question is about conformity to OCA theory. Regarding openness to trade, being a small economy, Hong Kong is tremendously more open than Argentina. Even though the specific linkage of goods trade with the United States for Hong Kong is not as large as that of Argentina, it is apparent that Hong Kong gains enormously from exchange rate fixity to the dollar due to its core competence in the business of financial services. On the symmetry of output variation and synchronicity of real interest rates, Hong Kong is clearly more convergent with the United States than Argentina. Meanwhile, both Hong Kong and Argentina have shown, in one way or another, greater price inflation convergence with the United States.

In brief, while studies highlighted at the beginning of this chapter, that is [1, 6, 7], Goodstadt [31], have pointed out the possible costs of the dollar-linked regime to the Hong Kong economy, the present findings appear to corroborate the prevailing Hong Kong arrangement and lend support to [2], which favors a fixed-dollar currency board regime for Hong Kong.

6. Conclusion

While the findings do lend support to the present currency board arrangement in Hong Kong, at most, the findings can only suggest that Hong Kong will not confront an Argentine-type breakdown of the currency board. Other possibilities posing threats to the sustainability of the currency board cannot be ruled out. Future studies may employ other available techniques to verify the findings and to explore other related facets, such as political and social dimensions.

In another respect, though the findings implicitly confirm the US dollar as the monetary anchor for Hong Kong, one must bear in mind the potential of using the Chinese renminbi as the anchor currency. For instance, Quah and Crowley [32, 33] have revealed evidence in favor of China as the monetary anchor country for Hong Kong. Recent events favoring this include efforts in internationalizing the renminbi by the People's Bank of China. These efforts encompass allowing cross-border payments in renminbi, direct currency swaps with close trading partners, and the establishment of an offshore market in Hong Kong where bonds denominated in renminbi are issued and traded. In light of this, future authors may consider China as an alternative monetary anchor country when investigating Hong Kong's currency board.

It is notable that the analysis focuses strictly on quantitative macroeconomic fundamentals and OCA criteria. Consequently, structural and political economy variables, such as the labor union rigidity in Argentina or the institutional credibility of the HKMA, are treated as exogenous factors. While these political dimensions are outside the scope of this quantitative framework, future research should integrate these institutional variables to provide a more holistic view of regime sustainability.

Author details

Chee-Heong Quah[1]* and Yew Joe Ho[2]

1 Faculty of Business and Economics, University of Malaya, Kuala Lumpur, Malaysia

2 University of Sanya, Hainan, China

*Address all correspondence to: quahch@um.edu.my

References

[1] Tam KP. A new comparative study on the free-floating and currency board regimes in Hong Kong. Bulletin of Economic Research. 2016;**68**(3):218–238

[2] Lo C. In defense of the Hong Kong dollar peg. The International Economy. 2013;**27**(2):59

[3] Ran J, Voon JP, Li G. How do oil price shocks affect a small non-oil producing economy? Evidence from Hong Kong. Pacific Economic Review. 2010;**15**:263–280

[4] Chen NF. The Hong Kong currency board during the 1997–8 crisis: Problems and solutions. International Review of Finance. 2001;**2**:99–112

[5] Goodstadt LF. The global crisis: Why Laisser-Faire Hong Kong prefers regulation HKIMR. Working Paper No.01/2010. Hong Kong Institute for Monetary Research; 2010

[6] Fung L, Yu I. Dislocations in the FX swap and money markets in Hong Kong SAR during The Global Credit Crisis of 2007–08. BIS Papers 54. Bank for International Settlement; 2010

[7] Devereux MB. A tale of two currencies: The Asian Crisis and the exchange rate regimes of Hong Kong and Singapore. Review of International Economics. 2003;**11**:38–54

[8] Imai H. Hong Kong's inflation and deflation under the US Dollar Peg: The Balassa-Samuelson effect or export price shocks? The Developing Economies. 2010;**48**:319–344

[9] Hanke Steve H. The Argentine straw man: A response to Currency Board Critics. Cato Journal. 2003;**23**(1):47–57

[10] Ho YJ. Stock Market Declines and Market Fundamentals. Kuala Lumpur: University of Malaya; 2017

[11] Ho YJ, Estrada Ruiz MA, Yap SF. The evolution of complex systems theory and The Advancement of Econophysics methods in the Study of Stock Market crashes. Labuan Bulletin of International Business & Finance. 2016;**14**:68–83

[12] Ho YJ, Estrada Ruiz MA, Yap SF. Examining the heterogeneous regimes of stock market identified with Two Variants of B-B algorithms that differ in rigidness of specification. Labuan Bulletin of International Business & Finance. 2017;**15**:32–41

[13] Artis M, Zhang W. Membership of EMU: A fuzzy clustering analysis of alternative criteria. Journal of Economic Integration. 2002;**17**(1):54–79

[14] Quah CH, Ho YJ. Is Brexit really supported? A view of optimal currency area. European Review. 2025;**33**(2): 155–174

[15] Hodrick RJ, Prescott EC. Postwar U.S. Business Cycles: An empirical investigation. Journal of Money, Credit and Banking. 1997;**29**(1):1–16

[16] Hanke Steve H. On dollarization and currency boards: Error and deception. Policy Reform. 2002;**5** (4):203–222

[17] Hanke Steve H. Why Argentina did not have a currency board. Central Banking Journal. 2008;**18**(3):56–58

[18] McKinnon RI. Rehabilitating the unloved dollar standard. SCID Working Paper. Stanford University: Stanford

Institute for Economic Policy Research; 2010

[19] Mundell R. A theory of optimum currency areas. American Economic Review. 1961;**51**:657–664

[20] McKinnon R. Optimum currency areas. American Economic Review. 1963;**53**:717–725

[21] Kenen P. A Theory of Optimum Currency Areas: An Eclectic View. In: Mundell RA, Swoboda AK, editors. Monetary Problems of the International Economy. Chicago: University of Chicago Press. 1969. p. 41–60

[22] Krugman P. Policy Problems of a Monetary Union. In: de Grauwe P, Papademos L, editors. The European Monetary System in the 1990s. Harlow: Longman. 1990. p. 48–64

[23] Quah CH. Exchange rate fixation between US, China, Japan and Eurozone. Margin-Journal of Applied Economic Research. 2017;**11**(2):99–120

[24] Quah CH, Ho YJ. Economic feasibility of Malaysia and Singapore-Brunei Monetary Reunion: A scrutiny during major financial crises. Applied Economics Journal. 2020; **27**(1):23–51

[25] Bayoumi T, Eichengreen B. Ever closer to heaven? An optimum-currency-area index for European countries. European Economic Review. 1997;**41**:761–770

[26] Gerlach S. World business cycles under fixed and flexible exchange rates. Journal of Money, Credit and Banking. 1988;**20**:621–632

[27] Baxter M, Stockman A. Business cycles and the exchange-rate regime. Journal of Monetary Economics. 1989;**27** (1):377–400

[28] Nguyen T. East Asian currency area: A fuzzy clustering analysis of homogeneity, development and policies research center working Paper No. 10. Vietnam: DPRC; 2007

[29] Fleming JM. On exchange rate unification. The Economic Journal. 1971;**81**:467–488

[30] Tavlas G. The "new" theory of optimum currency areas. The World Economy. 1993;**16**:663–685

[31] Goodstadt LF. Institute for Monetary and Financial Research, Hong Kong, China's Financial Reforms: Why Dysfunctional Banking Survives Research Paper WP No. 02/2012. 2012. DOI: 10.2139/ssrn.1988840

[32] Quah CH. Can Japan or China replace the US as the monetary anchor for Hong Kong and Macau? Asia Pacific Business Review. 2011. DOI: 10.1080/13602381.2011.608822

[33] Quah CH, Crowley PM. Which country should be the monetary anchor for East Asia: The US, Japan, or China? Journal of the Asia Pacific Economy. 2012;**17**(1):94–112